ABOUT THE AUTHOR

Jane Paterson held an Intelligence Commission in the WAAF during the last war and worked in photographic interpretation. She began studying Graphology nearly 40 years ago. She also completed courses in Child Psychology and Industrial Psychology and worked for a time as a social worker in a psychiatric hospital.

She is the co–author (with Brigadier Kennett and Noel Currer Briggs) of *Handwriting Analysis in Business* (ABP). After the publication of this book she held a series of seminars for business people on the use of graphology in personnel selection. She has been working steadily as a consultant in recruitment ever since.

She is the author of *Interpreting Handwriting* (Macmillan London) and *Know Yourself through Your Handwriting* (Readers Digest).

Patricia
With best wishes
from Jane Paterson

SIGN HERE
How Significant is Your Signature?

Jane Paterson

SIGN HERE

*How Significant
is Your Signature?*

ashgrove

ASHGROVE PRESS

Published by Ashgrove Press Limited
Bath Road, Norton St Philip, Bath BA3 6LW, UK

Distributed in the USA by
Words Distributing Company
7900 Edgewater Drive, Oakland
CA 94621, USA

A CIP catalogue record for this book is held
by the British Library

ISBN 1-85398-106-0

This book was designed and typeset
by Martyn James

Printed in Great Britain by Redwood Books Ltd
Trowbridge, Wiltshire

Contents

FOREWORD BY
PETER GABRIEL

I remember whiling away many hours of boring lessons at school trying to develop my own signature. The first time I ever asked anyone else for a signature was when I went in search of Peter Sellers' autograph. He was living at Elstead, a short bicycle ride away from my school. It required all the courage I then possessed to go up to the house and press the bell. A housekeeper emerged and agreed to ask the great man to sign. I was delighted to see him return carrying a piece of paper.

It was a trophy I was very proud of and I studied it frequently. I remember thinking it had just the right amount of confidence, direction, energy and pazazz to do whatever might be required of it. My signature, by contrast, seemed uncertain and insignificant (see page 123), something I thought I should and could take care of. I discovered that, although I could alter the size, direction and some flourishes, I couldn't seem to change the heart and feel of it. I didn't really understand why it was so difficult to do something else with it.

Around that time I would often visit a school friend, Rowley Paterson, to play tennis, to hang out, to swim and, increasingly, to talk about girls. His household struck me as very progressive, with lots of interesting and challenging conversation and a rare un–English openness. Rowley's mother was often hidden away in a room next to the kitchen doing something called 'graphology'. I had not come across many '–ologies' at that time and it aroused my curiosity.

I asked my parents, who were old friends of the Patersons, to explain graphology to me. My father, an electrical engineer, gave me my first understanding of the subject. He had a scientist's natural scepticism towards anything that could not easily be proven, and so I was much impressed by his willingness to take graphology seriously.

He was impressed with Jane's combination of analysis and insight and came to refer key employment decisions to her. I became very intrigued and have, in turn, sought Jane's advice on many important job decisions. I explain to those being considered why I am asking for handwriting samples, and offer mine in return. Only once have I been taken up on this offer, and then I was as curious, or as paranoid, as anyone else in trying to guess the results. I must admit that each time I send a hand–written letter to Jane, I wonder which of my secrets will be unravelled.

Like medicine, graphology can only be as good as its practitioners and, unfortunately, graphology, too, has it share of quacks and charlatans, who hinder the work of genuine researchers like Jane.

I am happy that Jane has put this book together, It is a fascinating introduction to all we reveal with a signature, that extraordinary creation of our public and private, conscious and unconscious selves.

Acknowledgements

The author would like to give special thanks to Peter Gabriel for his encouragement in the early stages of this book and for thinking of the title Sign Here. She would also like to thank Richard Cole who, when the project was stuck in the doldrums, provided inspiration and a new breath of life to see it through to completion. And she would like to thank John le Carré, Simon Weston. Dr Alistair Johnston and the pupils of the two schools who kindly contributed their signatures, and Jo Nicholl, Beryl Kearsey, Marty Stewart, Peter Marshall, Tony Morton, John Britten, Mary Paterson, Betty Lias, Lois Nut, Goldie Haller Williams and many others, for their help.

The author has been unable to trace the writers of some of the signatures that appear in this book, to ask their permission. Other signatures are so unusual or illegible that their provenance is unknown. The author would like to crave the indulgence of those whose signatures she has reproduced, and to take this opportunity to thank them.

Introduction

The arrival of a new baby in the family is a real beginning, a miracle of nature. Usually the first question asked is 'how much does the baby weigh?', followed by numerous oohs and aahs! and embarrassed observations. The next important question is 'what is the baby going to be called?' Visiting a baby who is a week or so old can be very disconcerting if the parents have not yet decided on a name. The baby seems in limbo, but as soon as a name is chosen, the child has an identity and is welcomed into the human family.

Our names are of vital importance to us, they are unique and from very early years we know they nominally distinguish us from other people. They are our identity, for better or worse. Children can suffer humiliation very early in life if they have unusual or unfortunate surnames. Roald Dahl in his book *Going Solo* writes of a man whose surname was Savoury but had the disadvantage of the initials U.N. Some names which have held the owner in good stead can suddenly become a problem. Being called James Bond in 1947 would have been fine, but as soon as the James Bond films came along it could be more than disconcerting.

There was a schoolmaster called Muirhead, a name which had served him well for many years and was, one would have thought, safe enough. But a few months after joining a new school he became Manurehead, and by the end of term his nickname was established as Dungnut!

It is important to feel happy with your name, as you have to travel with it all through your life. In these days of the break–up of families it can be difficult for a child to sustain a father's name if it has miserable associations. Sometimes a change of name can give a new start or 'rebirth'. Numerous people do in fact alter their names. Careers on the stage and in public life can be greatly assisted by a change of name.

The American President, Gerald Ford, was born Leslie Lynch King. Dame Margot Fonteyn, the famous ballerina, started life as Margaret Hookham. Elton John was Reg Dwight. Authors have often had pen names. David Cornwell is the well-known writer of spy thrillers under the pen name of John le Carré.

According to the *Oxford English Dictionary* the word 'signature' is the name or special mark of a person, written with his or her own hand, as an authentication of some document or writing. It is a compound of two words, 'sign' and 'nature'. 'Sign' is a gesture to convey a meaning; it is also a mark or token. The word 'nature' is the essential quality of a thing or person, or a person's innate qualities or character. From this we can deduce that a signature is a gesture or mark containing the essential innate qualities or character of the writer.

Your signature is also your name written down in the alphabet of your home language. It can be called your psychological identity card. It is entirely your own, manually produced and pictorially designed, both consciously and unconsciously, to suit your own taste. It represents your unique mark as an entity in your family and also your endorsement and personal seal to confirm whatever you stand for or wish to communicate to others and the outside world in general. It represents your 'Public Image'.

From very early times humans have found it important to have a written name or personal 'hall mark'. In the time before the birth of Christ, a name carved in stone in Egypt was called a 'Cartouche'. The dictionary tells us that a 'Cartouche' is an oblong panel enclosing characters expressing royal or divine names in Egyptian hieroglyphics.

Below is the Cartouche of an Egyptian Pharaoh, Ptolemy, who lived in the first Century BC. The characters representing the sounds which make up his name were carved in stone by a scribe.

Fig. 1

Cleopatra was the sister of Ptolemy: Below is her Cartouche. From this we find out that the lion stands for the sound 'l', the character 𓏏 for 'o' and the □ for 'p'. So even in the mist of history a name written down has individual significance for posterity

Fig. 2

Opposite is a facsimile of the sign manual of William the Conqueror (1027-1087). The cross would have been made by the King, the actual name being written by a scribe.

ɪ. Willelmus Rex.

Fig. 3

Below is a pictorial biography of Wingemund, a noted American Indian and Delaware Chief. No 1 on the picture is the tortoise totem of the tribe, No 2. is his 'chief totem' or individual mark, No 3 is the sun which shines on the strokes beneath. They represent the ten expeditions in which Wingemund took part. On the left of the picture, Nos 4, 5, 6, 7 are the prisoners taken, clearly indicated as either male or female, and also the number killed: these are drawn headless. In the centre of the picture, Nos 8, 9, 10. and 11 are sketches of the position attacked; and the slanting strokes at the bottom refer to the number of Wingemund's followers.

Fig. 4
Hernando Cortez (1485–1547), Spanish explorer, conqueror of Mexico. He lived by the sword, so it is not surprising that swords appear in his signature.

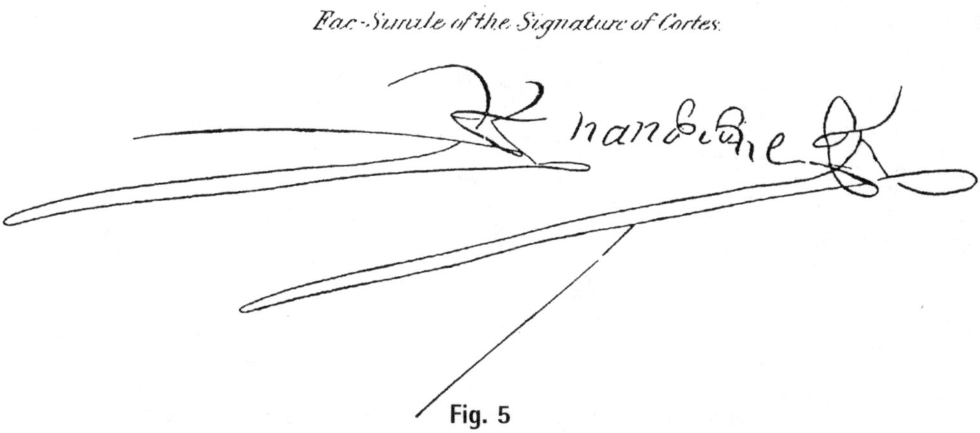

Fac-Simile of the Signature of Cortes.

Fig. 5

13

Below is the signature of Armand Jean du Plessis, Duc de Richelieu, French Statesman and Cardinal (1585–1642). A semblance of a sword appears as a finale to his signature.

Fig. 6

Below are signatures of King Alfonso XIII of Spain (1886–1941), and his wife Queen Victoria Eugenie, who was a niece of King Edward VII of England. Alfonso was the posthumous child of King Alfonso XII and may be said to have been King before he was born. A somewhat menacing, hard–line signature, with great depth, descending into the 'underworld'.

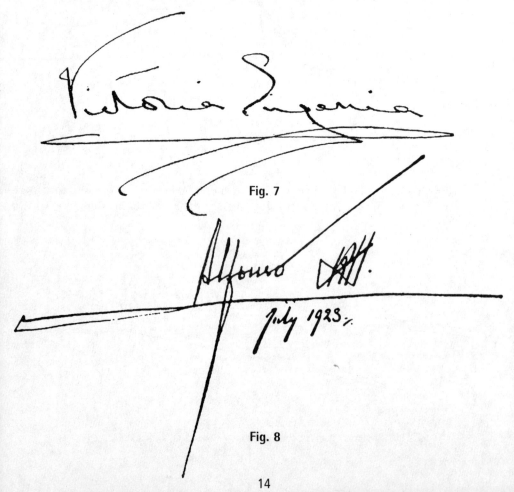

Fig. 7

Fig. 8

SIGNATURES OF THE ENGLISH ROYAL FAMILY FROM ELIZABETH I TO ELIZABETH II

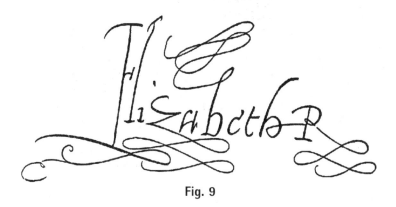

Fig. 9

Elizabeth I (1533–1603) famous Queen of England, intelligent daughter of Henry VIII and Anne Boleyn. In spite of many suitors she never married. **Fig 9** is her signature in 1561. Her signature has elaborate embellishments, mirroring the resplendence of her coiffure, ruff and jewel–encrusted finery.

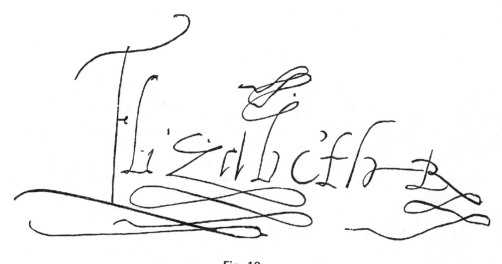

Fig. 10

This is her signature forty years later, in 1602. It is larger but the pen strokes are slightly shaky and not so perfectly executed as in 1561.

Fig. 11

George III, who came to the throne in 1760, was nicknamed 'Farmer George' because of the model farm he set up at Windsor. He and Queen Charlotte had nine sons and six daughters. Later in his reign he suffered from a disease called Porphyria. This signature was written in 1810, shortly before he ceased to discharge public duties. He lived in a pitiable state for ten more years.

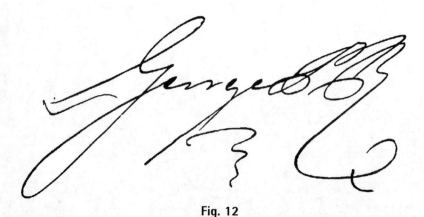

Fig. 12

His son George IV, born in 1763, became Prince Regent in 1810. Although he was notorious for extravagance and dissipation, the fantasy he indulged in to build the Royal Pavilion in Brighton is still attracting tourists to this day.

Fig. 13

Queen Victoria (1819–1901). The above was written when she was four.

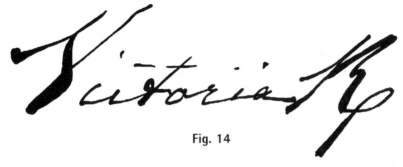

Fig. 14

Above, this strong signature was taken from the original on her coronation oath in 1837. Below, this was written in her later years after she had retired into seclusion. The large sweep of the 'V' over and down is a protective gesture.

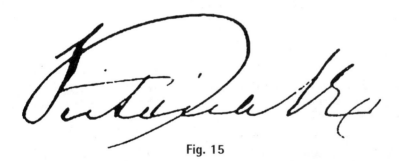

Fig. 15

Fig. 16
Victoria's eldest son Edward VII (1841–1910).

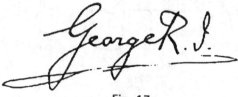

Fig. 17

George V (1865–1936) became King in 1910. Rather an old-fashioned country gentleman, popular with the general public.

Fig. 18

Edward VIII, later Duke of Windsor, abdicated because of his association with a divorcee, Wallis Simpson, whom he married. They remained together until his death.

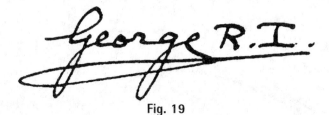

Fig. 19

George VI (1895–1952). He suffered from a stammer and never expected to become King. He and his wife were popular with the people. His signature is very similar to his father's.

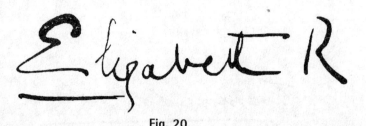

Fig. 20

Elizabeth II, became queen in 1952. This strong signature was taken from the original on her coronation oath.

Fig. 21

Her husband Prince Philip Duke of Edinburgh, 1952. Both these signatures are large, and upright.They both have poise, presence and self discipline.

Figs. 22, 23
Their signatures in 1986 have become smaller.

In order to understand more about signatures it seems important to know something about basic Graphology. Graphology is the study of human personality through the medium of handwriting. Graphologists have to start somewhere and they start where all writing starts, with a school copy book.

Since the dawn of time there seems to have been a continual wheel of change that turns: fashions emerge and become a part of culture. In their turn they become stale, decay, and then disappear back into the reservoir of happenings until their turn comes to re-enter the stage afresh and with new trappings.

Handwriting fashions, like those of costumes and architectural design, are continually changing and adapting. They are moulded and shaped by the social climate, collective choice and taste reflecting the 'expression' of the era and also by the technology of the day and materials available.

With the invention of pointed, pliable steel nibs in the later part of the 18th century and the increased needs of commerce and the law, came 'Copper Plate' **Fig. 24** This was a flowing, cursive writing, somewhat colourless, but nevertheless easy to read, quick to write and very suitable for clerks to keep records and produce detailed accounts.

The universal theme of the 19th and early 20th century copy-books was a flowing, connected writing with a rightward-moving slant, the tall uppers reaching up to the heights of ambition, the lowers putting down their materalistic roots.

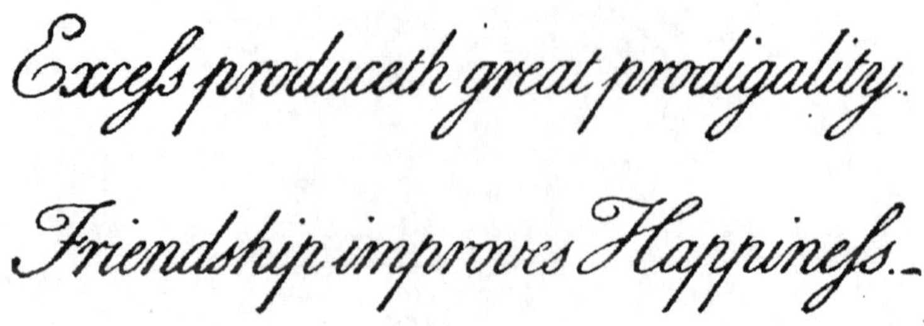

Excess produceth great prodigality.

Friendship improves Happiness.

JOHN BICKHAM, London, 1743

Fig. 24

These were the models for the people who went out into the world to shape the British Empire. They had high ideals, integrity and dedication. They consolidated their position and made money. The writing of Florence Nightingale **Fig. 25** shows the way she emanates this style, with her selfless devotion to service for others.

very faithfully Yours
Florence Nightingale

Fig. 25

Around the turn of the century Vere Foster introduced a new civil service copy-book and the pupil had to perfect his fluency, writing again and again sentences such as 'The poor man is often rich in kindness'; 'A generous action is its own reward'; 'Without frugality few can be rich'.

The years just before, during and after World War II, brought another significant change in writing forms. Although the Civil Service style continued as the pure descendent of the Copper Plate and some beautiful Italic styles still had their adherents, it was thought in Britain that it would be easier to combine the learning of reading and writing and 'print script' writing was then taught in the schools. **Fig. 26.**

Print script has no loops in the 'uppers' or 'lowers'. Later, a school mistress called Marion Richardson introduced a cursive style of joined-up writing but again, no 'loops'. It is interesting that early Graphologists said that loops in the 'uppers' indicated a love of children. The 20th century as it comes to its close has become a more 'loopless' society.

This writing was upright and disconnected and did not lend itself to cursive elegance. It was to herald the uncertain age of the common man, and technologically, the utilitarian, plastic, ball-point pen; the age of jeans, of specialisation, of dancing alone, gyrating individually, not proceeding or progressing with someone else in an ordered form. In ladies' clothes the vogue for

ABCDEFGHIJKLMNOPQRSTUVWXYZ
abcdefghijklmnopqrstuvwxyz

Print script alphabet in general use in primary schools

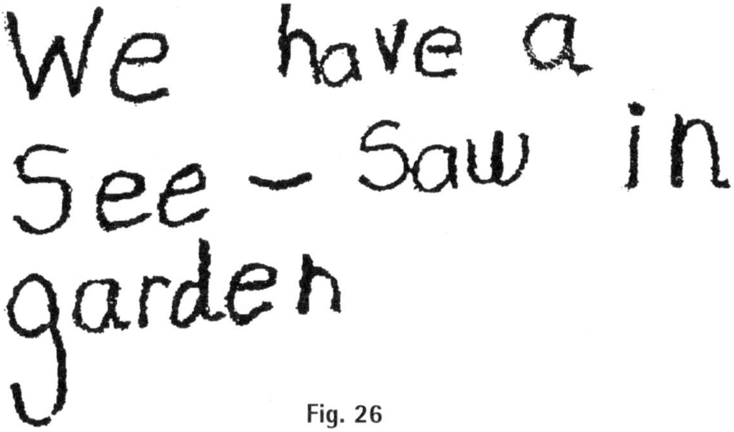

We have a
See - Saw in
garden

Fig. 26

'separates' surfaced where formerly there had been matching suits. The art world showed an abstract breaking up and away from conventional realism. In architecture, a time where bleak, soulless buildings rise up higher than church spires.

Copy books can start with different proportions but basically, writing can be divided into three different sections, the movements upwards away from the body, movements of the small letters along, laterally, and movements downwards towards the body. In the study of Graphology these are called:

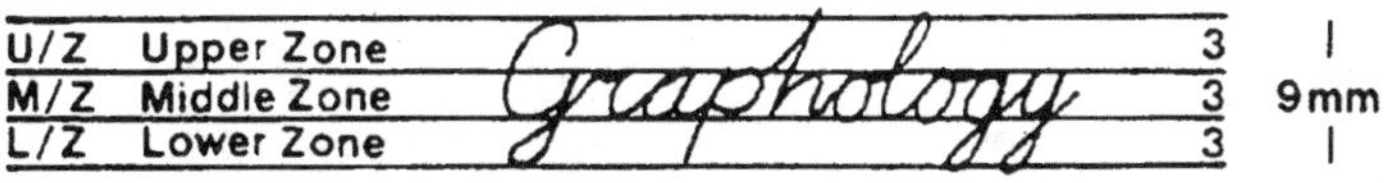

U/Z	Upper Zone		3	
M/Z	Middle Zone	*Graphology*	3	9mm
L/Z	Lower Zone		3	

Fig. 27

Every child in a class starts with the same copy book or writing model. Yet somewhere between the mental effort of the eye looking at the book or the blackboard and the manual, physical construction of the writing, the influence of the individual self is superimposed on the style. So from the very early stages the teacher knows John's writing because it is neat and tidy, Stephen's, because it is all over the place, and Billy's, because it is too big for the page.

Young people, early in life, take pains to master the manual control of writing their own names and get tremendous satisfaction from the achievement. Overleaf are the signatures, written in pencil, of a number of five year olds. Notice that each one, even at this stage, has its own individuality. Some have chosen to make their letters larger, some spread their names right across the page, others are more confined. Some space their letters nearer together, others further apart, but all have difficulty in aligning their letters.

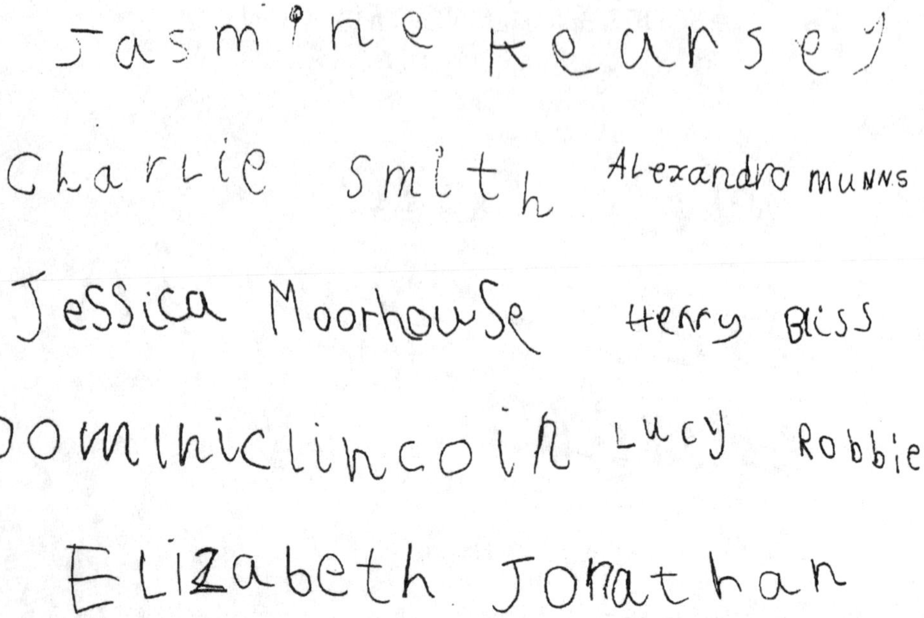

Jasmine Kearsey

Charlie Smith   Alexandra Munns

Jessica Moorhouse   Henry Bliss

Dominiclincoln   Lucy   Robbie

Elizabeth Jonathan

Fig. 28

Below are eight signatures of 8 to 9 year olds. The writing is now 'joined up' and written in ink. At this stage there seems a manual similarity or discipline to the signatures.

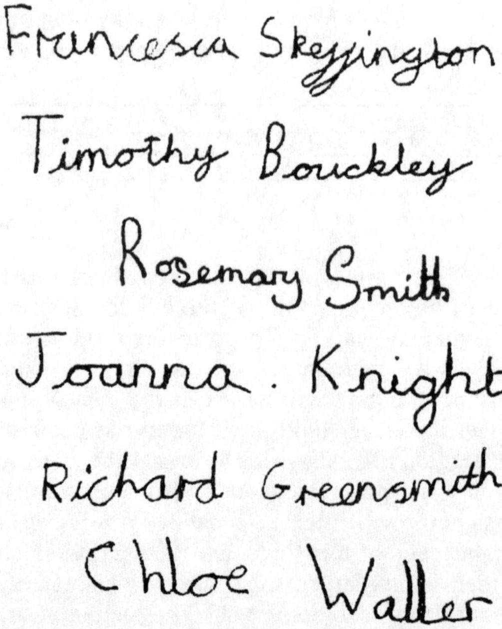

Francesca Skeffington

Timothy Bouckley

Rosemary Smith

Joanna . Knights

Richard Greensmith

Chloe Waller

Fig. 29

Below are the signatures of 12 year olds, starting to spread their wings and emerge into maturity. Personal style assumes more importance at this stage. They may incorporate into it elements of other writers in their family or some pop star idol of the moment. These are people they admire and want to absorb essence from, to become a part of themselves. No one ever copies someone they dislike, despise or look down on.

Fig. 30

Below are the signatures of 15 year olds. These are smaller, some very mature and sophisticated for their years

Fig. 31

All writing starts with a model to copy and the study of handwriting is based on these individual differences and how each person alters and adapts from the original copy-book. These changes from the model are governed by the individual's conscious and unconscious choice and, because personality is dynamic and not static, they will alter with and within the writing as a whole throughout life and according to the physical and mental well-being of the writer.

The writer should have reached a stage of writing maturity where attention is focused on the ideas and material put down on paper and not on the manual difficulty of forming letters. The writing flows along fluently.

Writing contains a number of dominant features, one of which is 'Size'. It can either be enlarged from the copy-book model or made smaller. Each dominant feature has a psychological implication, which will be influenced by the other dominants. Here, as we are dealing only with signatures, it is important to bear in mind that the signature is a 'Public Image'. It reflects the person's image of himself to the outside world, which can differ from what he thinks of himself privately.

Some people feel an inner need to have a very large signature, or Public Image. They want to be larger than life, they thrive on the oxygen of publicity, they can hold an audience and stand out in a crowd. They cannot fit into a small space.

Fig. 32   **Fig. 33**

Left signature: the large signature of an Estate Agent. Right signature: Clara Butt, a well-known singer who had a sense of 'presence' and could hold her audience. Small writers can have an inner sense of worth, are modest and do not like loud effects or self-display. They can fit into a small space.

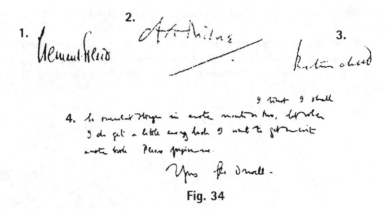

Fig. 34

(1) Clement Freud, TV personality, chef, talker for 'just a minute'.

(2) A.A.Milne, author of Christopher Robin books for children, 'thinking small'.

(3) Lord Rothschild.

(4) Minute writing of George Orwell. (whose real name was Eric Blair), author of *Animal Farm* (1945), and *Nineteen Eighty Four* (1949), in which he expresses mistrust of all political parties.

Another dominant feature in handwriting is 'Width'. The writer can either choose to make his letters broader than the copybook or narrower.

Fig. 35

(1) This is a powerful signature, but very narrow and restricted.

(2) Henry Alfred Kissinger, American statesman. His signature spreads itself out with no restriction. As Secretary of State he was a tireless traveller to all corners of the world. He was awarded the Noble Peace Prize in 1973.

Each feature has its own strengths and weaknesses and is affected by the other dominants. For instance, if a large writing is broad it accentuates 'release' and big heartedness, which can lead to extravagance. However, if the large writing is narrow, the 'think big' factor is restricted and may manifest itself in economy, thrift, or downright meanness.

Broad writing can dissipate energy and thus lose concentrated strength. Narrow writing contains strength but lacks breadth of vision, and so on.

Another feature of writing is the slant of the letters. In this country we write from left to right, so symbolically the left is where you have come from and the right is where you are going. Right slant writers tend to be more active and go ahead, they are aiming somewhere. Upright writers tend to be more neutral and reserved. Left slant writers, on the other hand, can stay more in their shells and be more defensive, leaning towards where they have come from.

Since 1721, when Sir Robert Walpole became the first Prime Minister, 53 men and one woman have held this high office. Out of these 54, 49 wrote their signatures with a right slant, five were upright. No one with a left slant signature has ever become Prime Minister: they are not so likely to be attracted to politics, much preferring to be historians, backroom advisers, etc.

In and since the post war period the country as a whole has become more 'left slant' and turned in on itself, focusing as never before on its past glories, and the tourist potential to be realised out of them. It has not yet found a goal out into Europe.

Fig. 36

The right slant writing of General Charles de Gaulle, a large man and a real leader of the French people.

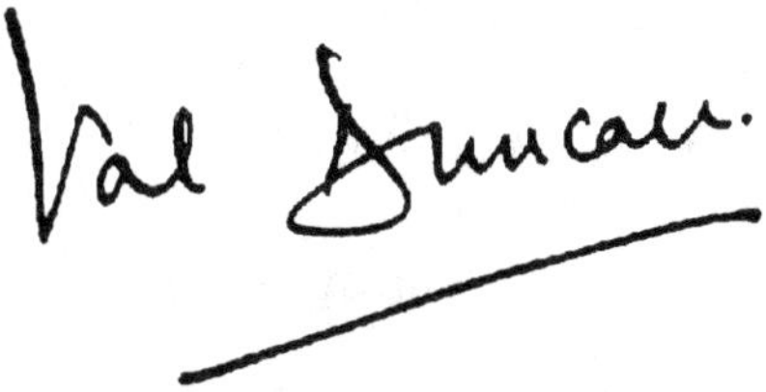

Fig. 37

Strong, legible, upright signature of a top business man.

Fig. 38

Strong, legible, slightly left slant.

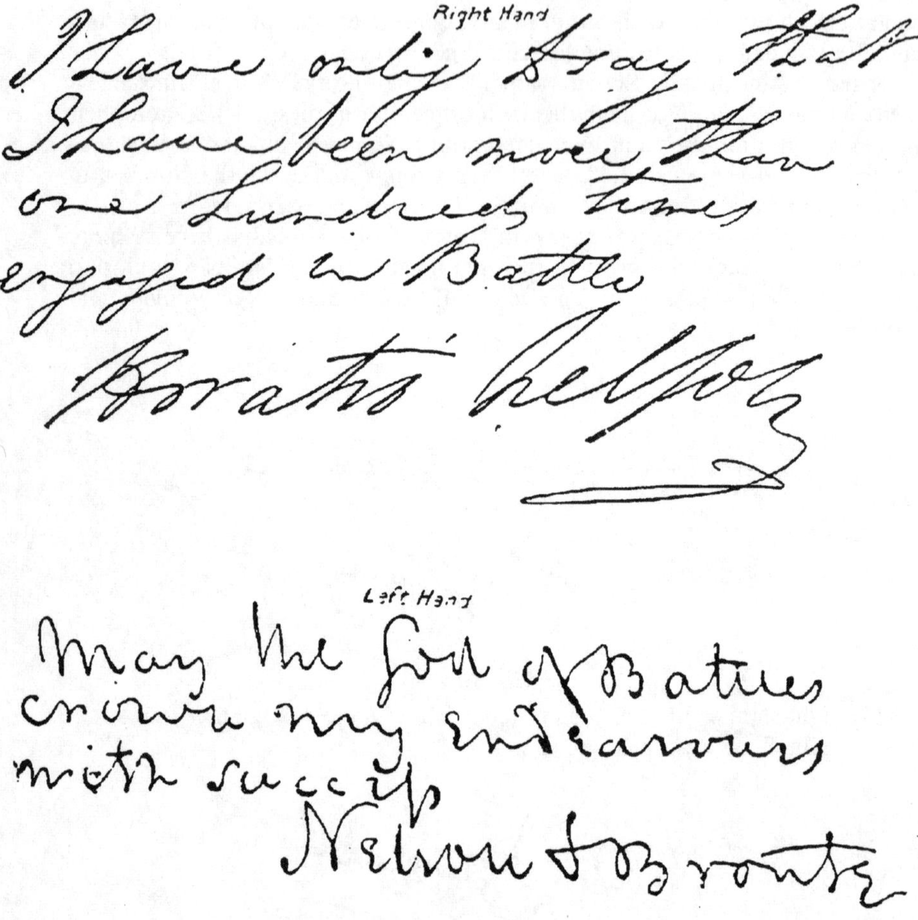

Right Hand

I have only to say that I have been more than one hundred times engaged in Battle

Horatio Nelson

Left Hand

May the God of Battles crown my endeavours with success

Nelson & Bronte

Fig. 39

Admiral Lord Nelson (1758–1805), hero, famous man of the sea, who lost his right eye while commanding a naval brigade in Corsica in 1797. He lost his right arm in an attack on Santa Cruz in Tenerife. He overcame this disability and learnt to write fluently with his left hand. The upper sample shows the active, right slant of his right handed writing. Below is the more passive left slant of his left handed writing. In both cases the signature is in keeping with the text.

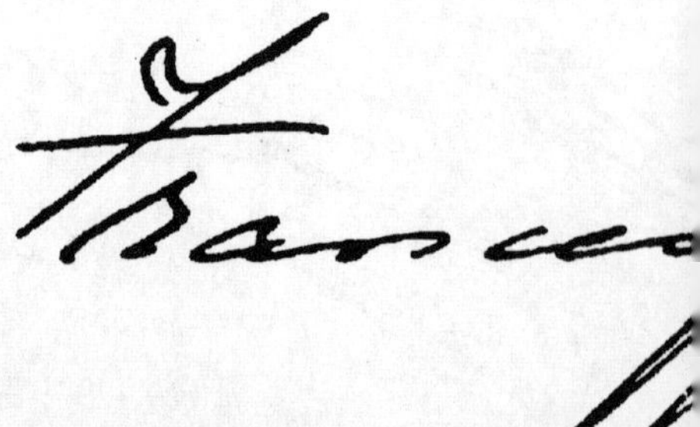

A writing can be right slant and narrow, in which case the outgoing of the right slant will be checked by inhibitions. Again,in a left slant writing that is broad, the outgoing breadth of vision will be protected by defensiveness. The essential thing in personality is harmony and balance.

The next dominant feature in handwriting is the Zonal Proportion. As mentioned before, Graphology is based on how people alter from the prescribed copy-book according to their own conscious and unconscious choice.

Writing can be divided into three sections or zones, the U/Z for movements upwards away from the body, the M/Z for movements of the small letters along laterally, and L/Z for movements downwards towards the body. Everyone starts with the three zones in proportion but few adhere to this.

Below is the signature of Frances Hodgson Burnett, author of the book *Little Lord Fauntleroy*. This signature must take up more space laterally than any other one. The zonal proportions are, exaggerated U/Z, very exaggerated L/Z. small M/Z(Fig. **40**).

The best way to illustrate the interpretation of the zones is to use the analogy of a tree. A tree has three zones: the top canopy branches reaching up to the sky, the middle trunk, which gives it strength, the roots of the tree which are unseen and underground but on which the tree draws for material nourishment.

The U/Z in writing represents aspirations upwards. We talk of living up to ideals, we lift up our hands in supplication, we think of the sky, the heavens from where help may come. The M/Z represents the here and now, the earth on which we walk, where we actually live and our social interactions. The L/Z represents the 'under world', the unconscious. We talk of getting down to business, we talk of people being earthy, we talk of mother earth and how when people die they return to the earth.

To return to the signature of Frances Hodgson Burnett, she has quite a high U/Z, so she is someone who has high aspirations and is generally high-minded, the M/Z is smaller in proportion, she is not self-centred, not much concerned with social comfort, or social dominance, there is a frugality in her social life. The L/Z sweeps down three times lower than any copy-book. Here we have a formidable business woman, earthy as well, in a very organised way. Conventional to the proprieties of her time, because the connection sticks to

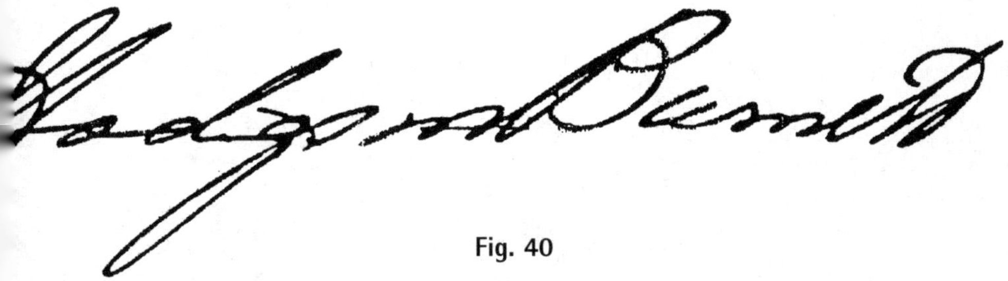

Fig. 40

the copy-book style; a bit strait laced, because the writing is fairly narrow. She needs a large house and space because the writing is also large. She is active and go ahead because the writing has a pronounced right slant. Not a shrinking violet, she would make an impact wherever she went.

Below we have a very different signature. It appears to be all M/Z, it has no uppers or lowers, but as the signature is illegible we do not know if it should have any, or who the writer is? He appears to be someone who is all concerned about power and social dominance in the here and now. Frances Hodgson Burnett lived much earlier, when people were high minded and bravely set off to new worlds to make their fortunes. It shows more the pattern of today, people being self-centred and over concerned with themselves.

Fig. 41

Whatever form of copy-book is used as a model, some people have a tendency to 'connect' their letters and some to leave then 'disconnected'. Again, this is a matter of personal choice.

Below is the signature of the Duke of Westminster. The capital 'W' at the start is large, so he makes an entrance. The writing is broad, the M/Z is small, and rather neglected, there is some thread and the letters tend to be disconnected. Here we are talking about the disconnection. People who write like this have an intuitive, jumpy way of thinking, can come up with new ideas and back hunches, they can, at times, be absentminded, because the writing is also broad, he is broad minded but can be wasteful. Because the M/Z is small, he tends to lack social confidence. This is a natural, unassuming signature; he appears to be a sensitive 'feeling' person.

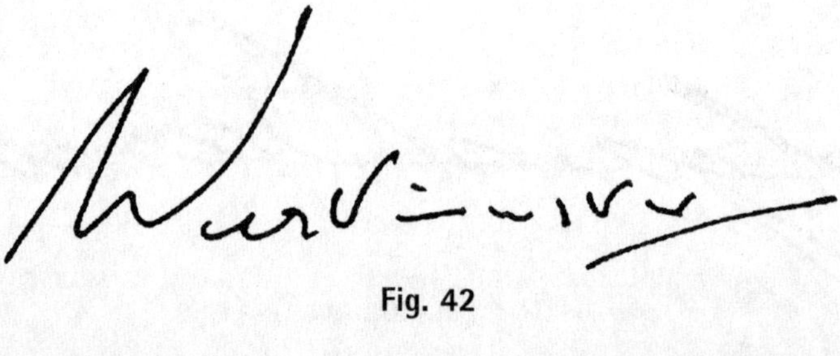

Fig. 42

Conversely, the signature of David Livingstone is connected. To 'connect' means to join together, link, show relationships between, associate, follow logically. The logical chain of thoughts can provide a solid barrier to new ideas, inspirations and hunches. Very connected writers can be blind to insight and 'feeling' for situations. They are sealed off from the unconscious, they can scoff at ghosts and premonitions.

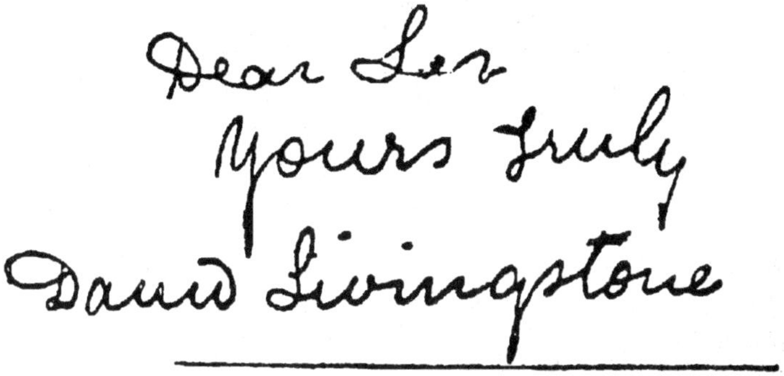

Fig. 43

David Livingstone, 1813 – 1873, was a Scottish missionary and explorer. He had worked for 14 years, from the age of 10, in a cotton mill, so he knew hard work and discipline. He explored central Africa and discovered the Victoria Falls. He wanted to press on again to find the source of the Nile. People would follow because he would generate confidence and surety. He would carry on come what may. One morning he was found dead. His followers must have thought very highly of him because, despite all the dangers of tropical Africa at that time, they brought his embalmed body to the coast and from there it was brought back to Westminster Abbey for burial.

FORMS OF CONNECTION

Another feature of handwriting is the way an individual chooses to connect his letters together. He can stick to a copy-book style, which is rounded and conventional..

Fig.44

Sir Edmund Gosse (1882–1928), English poet and critic.

The writer below chooses 'garlands'. These are round and curved, open like a cup, natural, flexible, receptive. Curves are thought of as feminine.

Fig. 45

The writer below uses 'threads' as a connection. These are formless, glide along quickly, avoid resistance, avoid decisions. This writer is Willy Brandt, Chancellor of Germany, 1969–1974, when he resigned. His name was former-ly Herbert Frahm. His signature is illegible, lacks all structure. He has no sure-ty or confidence in his name or in his 'Public Image' at the time of writing, but the writing has momentum towards a goal.

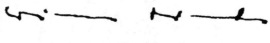

Fig. 46

Another possible way of connecting letters is with angles. They are hard and sharp, like an iron fence, rigid, decisive, inflexible. Angles are thought of as masculine. Most of the hard men in history prefer angles.

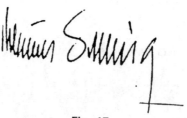

Fig. 47

Above is the signature of Helmut Schmidt, Chancellor of Germany from 1974–1982. A strong, steady, decisive signature, it has substance. The end stroke of the final 't' goes straight down. Writing is frozen gesture and this ges-tures is like putting your foot down and cutting people off sharply.

Having evolved a signature, the design usually remains fairly constant throughout the individual's life, depending of course on what happens to him or her. They can grow tremendously in importance and their signature can grow with them. They may have a break down, or an accident, which can be reflected in fractures, erosion and shrinkage in the signature, as their Public Image has become diminished and insecure.

The first name or forename of a signature is connected with a writer's early years and the private more intimate side of their life. The second name or 'surname' (not the 'sirename': the prefix means super or extra, like surcharge) is connected with their outside working life and 'Public Image'. Here, in a letter to the paper, the writer observes changes in the signature of Jeremy Isaacs.

JEREMY HAS, as I once predicted, finally gone — not from Covent Garden, but from the bottom of his letters.

I recently pointed out that the beleaguered General Director's signature has shrivelled over the last year from a firm "Jeremy I. Isaacs", to a "J-with-a-sort-of-wavy-line Isaacs" (without the I.) — well, last week his letter to the *Sunday Telegraph* denying that he is leaving the Opera House to return to television was signed like this:

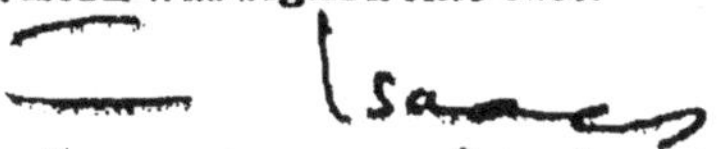

I am at a complete loss to explain the meaning of two straight lines. Are these changes significant?

Fig. 48

In this case 'Isaacs' is clear and firm, his public working life seems his all. The middle of the 'J' for Jeremy has disappeared, it has no centre or middle zone. This could indicate that his private, social life as Jeremy has been lost through his commitment to his work. No doubt this may be only temporary. Signatures frequently change through time, mirroring events in the individual's life.

When the first name of a signature is bold and legible but the surname dwindles or is completely illegible, it may indicate someone who is not at ease or has lost confidence in his or her public working situation, or has unfortunate associations with their father or a father figure whose name they hold. Again, it may be that they do not like their own name for some other reason. In the case of a married woman, she can be not altogether happy with her new name. The author was once playing in a golf, mixed foursome competition against a Mr and Mrs Freud. When the card was signed, by the wife at the end of the round, strangely the name signed on the card was not Freud. This was indeed a Freudian slip. It turned out that they had only been married for a fortnight.

Women have had to redesign and re-establish their signatures on marriage, but now with their own careers some prefer to keep their own names and their own signatures.

Some signatures are much smaller than the written text. In this case the writer wants the outside world to think he is more modest and self-effacing than is, in fact, the case.

Conversely if the signature is much larger than the text, the reverse is true. Here is someone who gives claim to being a much 'larger' personality in public, than he really estimates himself inside. He is putting on an act.

Other signatures can be 'stylised' in an artificial way and quite different from the script. Elaboration and accessories added to a signature can be like a garnish for effect.

These writers can be different people in public to the one they are in their own homes, playing a role in the way a Dictator can be a machiavellian man of great power, but changes to be a loving simple person when at home with his children.

Some people can decide to change their signatures when they retire, they no longer need the formal image they have adopted in their working life.

If you hold up a newly received hand-written letter and notice that your name is written fairly small, but the signature of the writer is twice the size, you will know in true comparison how the writer rates you in comparison with himself. Vice versa, if your name is very large and his signature is very small, you know the writer is someone who holds you in high esteem.

There are people who write their signature and then cross it through with their final stroke. If you ask them why they do it, some say 'perhaps I do not think much of myself'. The crossing through is a self negating or self destructive gesture.

Encouragement to boost their morale is vital, perhaps to suggest that they underline their signature instead. The author witnessed a considerable rise in the stature of a writer when someone noticed this stroke and kindly suggested the change.

There are times, however, when crossing out the signature is caused by serious illness. This writer was diagnosed as having terminal cancer, but boosting of morale can help fight adversity, however desperate.

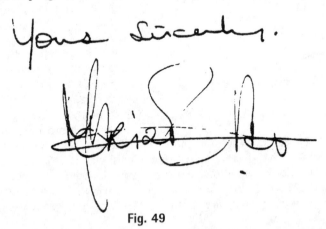

Fig. 49

There seem to be two main reasons why people take the trouble to write and yet write completely illegibly. One is that they do not want you to be able to read what they write, the other is that they do not care if you can read what they write. In general the same applies to signatures. One line of thinking is that an illegible signature can be a protection because it is more difficult to forge. Some writers may have an unconscious desire to escape from liability and actually being responsible for what they sign. Further, others have lost confidence in their place of work and their 'Public' standing. Television and 'Media' in general, have no doubt contributed to this pervading loss of face. It is very hard to keep up with the modern jet-setting Joneses.

Many people say that their signature is illegible because they have to sign so many things. This excuse does not really hold water because the really top people, who have surety in themselves, have legible signatures and they must sign thousands of papers.

An illegible signature is, in a way, being dismissive of others, a 'what the hell' attitude. But in doing this you are being dismissive of yourself and who you are. At present, there appears to be a vogue and one-upmanship in bizarre, illegible signatures. The writers probably like to bask in an aura of macho-mystery, but is there a vacuity to this? a pretence, an enigma, something to 'Hyde' behind?

BRITISH PRIME MINISTERS
FROM SIR ROBERT WALPOLE TO LORD JOHN RUSSELL

1. Sir Robert Walpole
(1721-1742)

2. Spencer Compton
(1742-3)

3. Sir Henry Pelham
(1743-54)

4. Duke of Newcastle
(1754-6, 1757-62)

5. Duke of Devonshire
(1756-7)

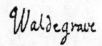

6. 2nd Earl Waldegrave
(1757)

7. Earl of Bute
(1762-3)

8. George Grenville
(1763-5)

9. Marquess of Rockingham
(1765-6, 1782)

10. William Pitt the Elder
(1766-7)

11. Duke of Grafton
(1767-70)

12. Frederick, Lord North
(1770-82)

13. 2nd Earl of Shelburne
(1782-3)

14. 3rd Duke of Portland
(1783, 1807-9)

15. William Pitt the Younger
(1783-1801)

**16. Henry Addington,
1st Viscount Sidmouth**
(1801-4)

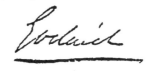

17. Lord Grenville
(1806-7)

18. Spencer Perceval
(1809-12)

19. 2nd Earl of Liverpool
(1812-27)

20. George Canning
(1827)

21. Viscount Goderich
(1827-8)

22. Duke of Wellington
(1828-30)

23. 2nd Earl Grey
(1830-4)

24. 2nd Viscount Melbourne
(1834, 1835-41)

25. Sir Robert Peel
(1834-5, 1841-6)

26. Lord John, Earl Russell
(1846-52, 1865-6)

BRITISH PRIME MINSTERS
FROM THE EARL OF DERBY TO TONY BLAIR

27. 14th Earl of Derby
(1852, 1858-9,1866-68)

28. 4th Earl of Aberdeen
(1852-5)

29. 2nd Viscount Palmerston
(1855-8, 1859-65)

30. Benjamin Disraeli
(1868, 1874-80)

31. W.E. Gladstone
(1868-74, 1880-5, 1892-4)

32. 3rd Marquess of Salisbury
(1885-6, 1886-92, 1895-1902)

33. 5th Earl of Rosebery
(1894-5)

34. A.J. Balfour
(1902-5)

35. Sir Henry Campbell-Bannerman
(1905-8)

36. H.H. Asquith
(1908-16)

37. David Lloyd George
(1916-22)

38. A. Bonar Law
(1922)

39. Stanley Baldwin
1923-4, 1924-9. 1935-7)

40. J. Ramsay MacDonald
1924, 1929-31, 1931-35)

41. A Neville Chamberlain
(1937-40)

42. Winston Churchill
(1940-5, 1951-5)

43. C.R. Attlee
(1945-51)

44. Anthony Eden
(1955-7)

45. Harold Macmillan
(1957-63)

46. Sir Alec Douglas-Home
(1963-4)

47. J. Harold Wilson
(1964-70, 1974-6)

48. Edward Heath
(1979-4)

49. James Callaghan
1976-79)

50. Margaret Thatcher
(1979-90)

51. John Major
(1990-97)

52. Tony Blair
(1997-)

1. Arthur Scargill

President of the National Union of Mine Workers. A two tier signature; Arthur is legible, written above, and has tow 'pride of achievement' loops, one on the 't' cross, one at the foot of the 'A'. Scargill is below, not legible, part crossed through. This is a dynamic signature, rising, and there is a sort of 'rocket' propelling i into the future.

2. Tony Benn

Rising up, irrepressible, a small, angular signature.

3. David Mellor

A strong signature, but quite illegible. We do not know who he is.

4. Ann Widdecombe

Formidable, needs to protect herself; uses final enrolment, feels things are against her.

5. Paddy Ashdown

Seems rather choked and squeezed up.

6. Kenneth Clark
Former Chancellor, seems in too much of a hurry.

7. Roy Jenkins
As strong, small, legible signature

8. Chris Patten
A strong, right-slant signature.

9. Michael Heseltine
A large signature, but lacks core strength

10. J. Enoch Powell
An outstanding mind and a controversial politician. Classicist, Professor of Greek at the University of Sydney (1937-9), he joined the British army as a private and rose during the Second World War to the rank of Brigadier. He speaks and reads several European languages, is a theologian and is fluent in Medieval Welsh. His post-war career as Conservative politician and minister was marked by the power of his public speaking and the controversy he aroused. He is courteous, hardworking; perhaps too direct, forthright, logical to succeed in democratic politics?

1. Jawaharlal Nehru

(1889-1964), first Prime Minister of India.

2. Martin Luther King

(1929-1968), American Civil Rights leader, awarded the Nobel Peace Prize. Notice the stroke in his signature: it goes down, makes the loop, swings to the left and then comes back to cross through the name 'King' from left to right. Perhaps a premonition of the way his devotion to the cause could destroy his life.

3. Nelson Mandela

ANC leader, President of South Africa, a signature mellowed in old age.

4. Valéry Giscard d'Estaing

Former President of France.

5. Konrad Adenauer

(1876-1967), Chancellor of Germany.

6. Eamon de Valera

(1882-1975), President of the Irish Republic.

May God bless you in your home

Basil Hume

1. Cardinal Basil Hume
Archbishop of Westminster

2. *J. L.*
A clergyman.

6. Bishop Trevor Huddleston
Former missionary in South Africa,
who wrote Naught for your Comfort.

Trevor Huddleston Cr

Sue Ryder   *Lenard Cheshire*

3. & 4. Sue Ryder,
Selfless worker for charity and her late husband, **Group Captain Leonard Cheshire.**

Helen Keller

5. Helen Keller
(1880-1968). This remarkable woman became deaf and blind as a result of scarlet fever when she was 19 months old. Through the dedication of her teacher she learned to talk and write. She went on to get a degree and become an author and lecturer. The letters stand out clearly, but they look lonely and detached.

Robert St Albans

7.
Robert Runcie, former Archbishop of
Canterbury, when Bishop of St Albans.

All the Presidents of the USA have a right slant to their signatures except John Quincy Adams and Lyndon Johnson. Johnson succeeded to the Presidency rather than being elected. Would Adams have become President if his father had not held that office before him?

1. George Washington

(lived 1732-1799), First President of the United States of America. When he died he was said to be 'First in war, first in peace and first in the hearts of his countrymen'.

2. John Adams

(1735-1826), First Vice-President and Second President, he signed the Declaration of Independence. His signature has very large M/Z letters.

3. John Quincy Adams

(1767-1848), Sixth President, the eldest son of John Adams. His signature is the smallest of any US President. He was fiercely motivated to fight against the wrongs of slavery. Small writers tend to identify with the less fortunate.

4. William Henry Harrison

(1773-1841), Ninth President, he died within a month of taking office.

5. Abraham Lincoln

(1809-1865), the 16th President. He proposed a policy 'With malice towards none, with charity for all'. Five days after the end of the Civil War he was shot in a Washington theatre by the actor John Wilkes Booth.

6. James Abram Garfield

(1831-1881), a lawyer from Ohio, was the 20th President. He was shot in Washington, DC four months after his inauguration.

7. William McKinley

(1843-1901), 25th President. He was killed by an anarchist at Buffalo station shortly after being elected President for the second time.

8. Theodore Roosevelt

(1858-1919), 26th President. He became President after the assassination of McKinley and was said to use his power more vigorously than any President since Lincoln.

9. John Calvin Coolidge

(1872-1933), 30th President. A very sharp, angular signature, he would have been acutely curt and incisive.

10. William Jefferson Clinton

(b.1946), 42nd President.

THE STAGE 1922

1. Dame Sybil Thorndike

2. Sir John Martin-Harvey

3. Maud Tree

4. Sir Charles Hawtrey

5. Irene Vanbrugh

6. Henry Ainley

THE STAGE - LATER

7. Jane Asher

8. Sir Alec Guinness

9. Sir John Gielgud

10. John Hurt

11. Robert Hardy

12. Susannah York

13. Gemma Jones

14. Maria Aitken

THE STAGE: ILLEGIBLE

1. Sir Peter Ustinov

English actor, playwright of Russian descent; Illegible, enigmatic, artistic, grandiose curves, but no M/Z substance.

2. Albert Finney

A talented actor, quite high initial letters but no M/Z strength.

3. Michael York

Another talented actor, illegible, no M/Z strength, dislikes publicity

4. Susan Hampshire

A lovely-looking, talented actress, no M/Z solidity. It is known that she triumphed over great adversity with dyslexia.

5. Eleanor Bron

Another talented actress but her signature is a bit of a mess.

6. Larry Grayson

Comedian. Curves in three directions are indicative of humour. His 'public image' looks vulnerable.

THE STAGE: LEGIBLE

7. Alan Whicker

TV Travel Journalist, irrepressible, rising up, larger than life, enjoys publicity.

8. Robert Powell

Large U/Z, high aspirations, a strong signature.

9. Alan Bates

Legible, strong signature, clever simplifications of letters.

10. Paul Eddington

Legible, cultured.

11. Sir Peter Hall

Legible and solid.

12. Peter Sellers

Legible, marked active right slant, unstoppable.

1. Spencer Tracy
(1900-1967)
American Actor; he made 72 films, won two Academy Awards, co-starred with Katherine Hepburn. He places Spencer above Tracy; stylish down stroke of the 'P' in Spencer to firm the 'T' for Tracy The M/Z has become a formless thread and the bottom of the 'y' is crossed through. Was his private life an unconscious anguish to him?

2. Terence Stamp
Actor, good-looking, a very similar signature to the above with unfulfilled M/Z.

3. Elvis Presley
(1935-1977)
American rock and roll singer, film star, a real heart–throb and cult figure. 'Sex symbol' appears in the U/Z, but the large left loop in the L/Z swings to the left, where he has come from, his mother. She undoubtedly had a powerful influence over him unconsciously.

4. Elizabeth Taylor
English film actress, child star, a celebrated beauty. She married Mike Todd, Eddie Fisher, Richard Burton twice, among others. Very similar to the above signature in style but a large, inflated grab hook appears on the L/Z.

5. James Cagney
American film star. His L/Z loops are crossed through.

6. Bob Hope
Larger than life American film star, comedian, he made films with Bing Crosby.

7. Rock Hudson
American film star.

8. Charlton Heston
Tough guy, American film star.

9. Robert Taylor
American film star

1. Gladys Cooper
Actress earlier this century. Large, dynamic, rounded writing

2. Marilyn Monroe
(1926-1962)
American film star and sex symbol

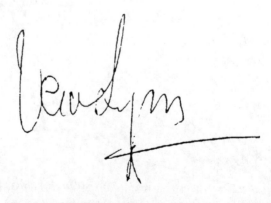

3. Brigitte Bardot
French film star and sex symbol

4. Vera Lynn
Singer, the forces sweetheart in World War II

Nellie Melba 1923

5. Nellie Melba
(1861-1931)
Australian soprano

Audrey Hepburn

6. Audrey Hepburn
American film star, a small signature, not publicity-seeking.

Greta Garbo of my heart

7. Greta Garbo
Swedish actress, she shunned publicity, and 'wanted to be alone'

Vesta Tilley de Frece

8. Vesta Tilley
(1864-1931)
Lady de Frece, one of the greatest stars of the music hall, a male imperson-
ator; her writing is large and angular and the stroke of her writing is sharp
or 'thin', indicating an astute critical sense.

1. Charlie Chaplin
(1889-1973)

He knew extreme poverty and hunger as a child. It was this 'poor thing' image that he cultivated with its unique humour in the early silent films. The signature looks gaunt and harsh. Humour can be a safety valve of compressed hardship. Most clowns are sad.

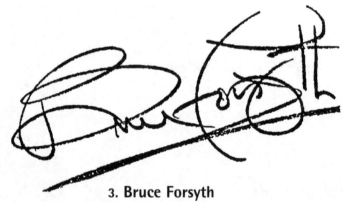

2. Sammy Davis Junior
Very talented American singer and dancer, also emerged to stardom from hardship. A disturbing signature: rather violent angles, roofed over for protection.

3. Bruce Forsyth
Belongs with the dancers, lots of movement and verve, panache, lovely curves.

4. Michael Crawford
This is a sad 'public image'. He does not like publicity. The M/Z is very undernourished; he lacks social confidence. Immensely talented, hardworking perfectionist, he has given such pleasure to thousands.

5. Jasper Carrot

A really bumptious signature, larger than life, voluptuous curves, irrepressible.

6. Kenny Everett

TV personality. Notice how the 'y' of Kenny cuts through the symbolism in the 'E' of Everett and the end 't' crosses backwards through his signature.

7. Noel Edmonds

Rising up optimistically, large triangle in the L/Z.

8. Sir Noel Coward

(1899-1973)

He makes the same down stroke with his 'l' as 6, cutting through the 'Coward', a dreadful name to live up to. Then he adds a stylish protective loop to guard himself.

1 & 2

Different signatures of Spike Milligan, well-known actor, comedian, one of the Goons, unique, zany style of humour.

3. Brian Rix

Actor well-known for his 'Whitehall' farces.

4. Lady Isobel Barnett

TV star of 'What's my Line?' A small signature, with a strange, aggressive stroke towards the past in the L/Z

5. Frank Muir

TV star A rather old-fashioned signature in keeping with his bow-ties.

6. Dennis Norden

TV star, now well-known for his sharp wit and out-takes.

7. John Cleese

A rather tortuous signature for this writer, actor and comedian, mirroring the convoluted postures he manages to produce.

8. Malcolm Muggeridge

Journalist, correspondent, witty, versatile, controversial. The 'ridge' has vanished from his signature.

9. John Mortimer

Barrister, author, playwright , creator of 'Rumpole'

10. Sir Mortimer Wheeler

(1890-1976)
Well-known English archaeologist, keeper of the London Museum, TV star.

11. Sir John Betjeman

(1906-1984)
English writer, Journalist, poet laureate; very flattened M/Z, shows lack of social self-assurance; he could always laugh at himself.

12. Bamber Gascoigne

Academic, author, TV Quiz Master of University Challenge. Initially inflated but meagre M/Z lacks core strength inside.

1. Felicity Kendal

2. Griff Rhys Jones

3. Angela Rippon

4. Michael Fish
Weatherman,
BBC and Meteorological Office

5. Shirley Bassey CBE

6. Esther Rantzen OBE

7. Ned Sherrin

8. Antony Sher

9. Sir Anthony Hopkins

Michael Jackson's strong, legible signature, from his biography *Moonwalk* (1988) is reproduced here. He was the seventh of nine children, living in a three room house. In the 'M' of Michael, notice that the first point is very low and the second is very high. Hans Jacoby, in his book *Self-Knowledge through Handwriting*, calls this the frog's eye view, the position of someone who is 'down'and determined or fired by ambition to climb up. The converse is the 'M' of condescension, looking down on other people from an exalted position. This latter is the snob's 'M'.

Michael's signature is disciplined and clear, executed with fluency and precision. It has angles which are hard in the way an iron fence is hard; angles are 'masculine'. The signature also contains beautiful curves which are 'feminine'. The perfect curve of the 'l' at the end of Michael encircles the 'J' of Jackson and forms the central focus of the signature. In the old days the copybooks prescribed a good loop to the letter 'l', but after World War II print script was taught in the schools. This had no loop to the 'l'. Families became smaller, Society has become less child oriented. Early graphologists said that an 'l' with a rounded loop was found in the writing of people who liked children. Michael has said that he lost his own childhood because he was always working and there was never time to play.

To balance the end of the signature the 'n' flies up in a sharp angle. At the conclusion of the down stroke there is a star. Michael became a great one, but this star has fallen below the base line. This seems inevitable in the design of the signature, to counter-balance his over-fired ambition.

Nowadays many people enhance their signatures by adding objects, symbols, signs, of themselves, their interests or their careers.

1 & 2.

The brilliant animators who conceived and brought the Muppets to life. **Frank Oz (1)** writes Miss Piggy's signature as he thought she would write it. Then **Jim Henson** signs for Kermit the Frog, and for himself underneath.

3. Liberace

The singer skillfully outlines his grand piano and candelabra.

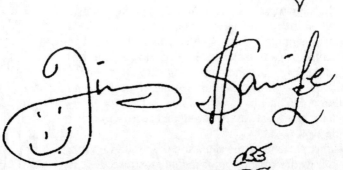

4. Sir Jimmy Saville OBE

Tireless in his pursuit of funds for those less fortunate, he adds dollar and pound signs and smiling face.

5. Bill Oddie

His interest in wildlife is well known. Here he puts in a few birds for good measure.

6. Ellis Parker Butler

The American author draws a cute little pig.

7. Leslie Charteris

The author of the 'Saint' book, whose detective was Simon Templar, adds a small sketch of the Saint.

8. Sir Gerald Nabarro

The late British Member of Parliament, easily recognised by his handlebar moustache, incorporated it in his signature!

SOME FLOURISHES AND COMPLICATIONS

1. Joan Crawford

Actress, film star. Extremely large, fluent, flowing writing; someone who steps over limits. Joan is fairly legible, but Crawford ends up in a strange convolution.

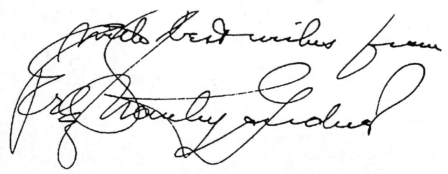

2. Erle Stanley Gardiner

American writer with a prodigious output of cleverly woven detective stories. His signature is fluent, but it seems to get embroiled and entwined in a web of flourishes and complications. Probably his thrillers follow a similar twisting path of false trails and meanders to throw the reader off the scent until the final revelations.

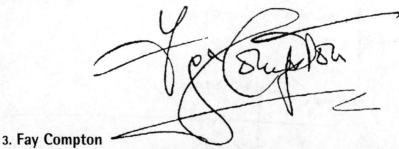

3. Fay Compton

Actress. Another flourished and complicated signature. All the above were large personalities.

1. Albert Einstein
1879-1955, physicist, famous for his general theory of relativity.

2. Sir Barnes Wallis
Designer of the bouncing bomb used against the Mohne dam in W War II.

3. Sir Robert Watson Watt
Scottish physicist, pioneer of Radar in W War II.

4. Alexander Fleming
Scottish Bacteriologist discoverer of penicillin.

5. Lord Rutherford
British physicist, born in New Zealand, won the Nobel prize for chemistry.

6. Frank Whittle,
Pioneer of jet propulsion.

7. Bertrand Russell
English philospher and mathematician.

8. Oliver Lodge
Physicist.

9. G Marconi
Italian physicist and inventor, credited with the first practical system using radio for signalling.

1. Frank Lloyd Wright

(1869-1959), original American architect. He stressed the importance of a harmonious relationship between his buildings and the landscape they were set in.

2. Edwin L. Lutyens

(1869-1944), famous English architect, President of the Royal Academy.

3. Peter Cheyney

The writer has a strong, ornate, artistic signature.

4. Tom McNab

The athlete is running speedily.

5. Mark Twain

Pen name of the American **Samuel Langhorne Clemens** (1835–1910). The author of *Tom Sawyer* and *Huckleberry Finn* took his name from his time as a Mississippi river pilot: the leadsman's cry 'Mark Twain' indicated that the water was two fathoms deep.

6. Lord Byron

George Gordon Noel, sixth Baron Byron (1788–1824), English Romantic poet. After an unhappy childhood, his writing made him famous. He certainly had to protect himself, as his amorous adventures caused scandal. He uses a protection stroke to cross through his 'surname'.

7. Patrick Moore

British expounder on astronomy.

8. Yul Brynner

The film star's signature is very enigmatic.

9. Rudolf Hess

(1894–1987), German Nazi politician, who flew to Scotland in 1941, apparently on an unauthorised peace mission. 'Rudolf' is clear and starts with a large 'R'. The word rises up, but the signature declines in an arc. The capital 'H' of 'Hess' is small and the name falls right down.

10. Walt Disney

(Walter Elias, 1901–1966). The Two signatures of the American cartoon producer: **(a)** a formidable, complicated signature; **(b)** another variety, M/Z importance emphasised with capital letters.

All these signatures are clear and legible. the writers' jobs demand that they are reliable, have presence and poise, and can speak clearly.

1. Henri Toulouse-Lautrec

(1864-1901), French painter. Crippled by a fall from a horse, he grew up a stunted dwarf. Note the odd deformation which appears in the L/Z of the signature.

2. Pablo Picasso

(1881-1973), Spanish artist, associated with cubism and surrealism.

3. Claude Monet

(1840-1926), French Impressionist.

4. Salvador Dali

(1904-1989), dadaist and surrealist.

5. Camille Pissaro

French Impressionist.

6. L.S. Lowry

(1887-1976), whose style, depicting matchstick figures and factory scenes, was unique.

The Impressionist had exquisite use of colour and sensuality. One would expect them to have a thick stroke to their writing and to have disconnected letters. Their pictures were often composed of dabs and spots, not washes of paint. One would also expect the surrealists to have disconnected writing, to enable their unusual ideas to emerge. the signature of the British artist, L.S. Lowry, is so different: he was a civil servant, and enjoyed being one

1. Frederick Ashton

Succeeded Ninette de Valois as Director of Sadlers Wells Ballet. A wonderful signature: control, ballet 'positions' with movement.

2. Vaclav Fomich 'Nijinsky'

Russian ballet dancer and choreographer, he is remembered as one of the greatest male dancers of all time.

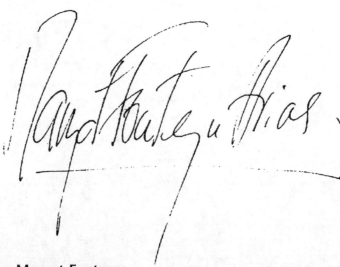

3. Dame Margot Fonteyn

Prima Ballerina of the Royal Ballet, she partnered Rudolf Nureyev after his arrival in the West.

4. Rudolf Nureyev

Leading dancer of the Kirov Ballet, this signature was written when he first defected to the West. It is a medley of ballet shoes.

5a & b Fred Astaire and Ginger Rogers

They just belong together in movement in their signatures as in their dancing. One can feel the swish of her skirt and the controlled elegance of them moving in unison. Their writing style is so similar; they had a unique affinity.

6. Sir Robert ('Bobby') Helpman

The Australian leading male dancer of Sadlers Wells, doing a stunning pirouette with his pen.

1. Prince Otto von Bismarck

(1815-1898), German statesman and Field-Marshall. A very important figure in German history.

2. Paul von Hindenburg

(1847-1934), German Field Marshall and President; a popular father figure throughout the first world war.

3. General Franco

(1892-1975), Spanish leader and dictator.

4. Major General Sir F. Sykes, MP

It looks as if he is firing a gun!

5. Fidel Castro Ruz

Cuban politician, communist dictator.

6. Juan Domingo Peron

(1895-1974), President of Argentina.

7. Benito Mussolini

(1883-1945), Dictator of Italy

8. Heinrich Himmler

(1900-1945). A German poultry farmer who became a Nazi politician, then head of the secret police, the Gestapo. This is a very frightening signature. Firstly, it is large, so we have someone who needs to be important. The letters are narrow, so he is inhibited, narrow-minded, 'shut in'. Again, the letters are extremely angular, so he is hard, rigid, inflexible, merciless. There is a very large M/Z, which is about social power, domination over others; also the letters are all connected, so he is 'closed', no feeling or intuition. No milk of human kindness runs in his veins. The rising cross strokes on the two capital 'H's rise up like stiff Nazi salutes.

10. Erwin Rommel

German Field Marshall, he gained the highest decoration for valour in World War I. He commanded the Afrika Corps in the North African desert in World War II. It is not certain if he died form injuries or was ordered to commit suicide because of suspected complicity in the bomb attempt on Hitler's life.

9. Earl Kitchener

Field Marshall and subsequently Earl. He was also an engineer, with a knowledge of arabic and hebrew. In the Boer war made reforms in hygiene and sanitation. Kitchener and Rommel have strong signatures, but they both connect their letters with 'garlands': they have a receptiveness to humanity.

11. Adolf Hitler

(1889-1945), German Dictator.

12. General Sir Alex Godley

General in World War I.

GHLeigh·Mallory

J·M·L·Noel·

T. Howard Somervell

CGBruce

EL Strutt

Arthur W Wakefield

[signature]

John Hunt

There seems a strong spiritual dimension in the lure of high mountains to climbers: there is a mystique and grandeur up there which is heady. Humans have always looked up to the heavens for help and inspiration. If you look at these signatures you will see that the first two have a slight quality of rising up, the third has a marked U/Z, the fourth has an underlining going up, the fifth a rising 't' cross, the sixth a rising 't' cross, the seventh a very dominant U/Z.

The last signature is that of **Sir John Hunt**, British soldier and mountaineer, who subsequently led the first successful ascent of Everest, in 1953, though not himself reaching the summit. His signature also rises up and finally the 't' cross goes even higher: in front he carries a flag to plant on the summit.

Above, the signature of Simon Weston, British hero of the Falkland War. He has shown tremendous courage in his fight back to life. he must have suffered more than anyone can imagine and yet he says he hopes it is not dismissive to other people that his signature is illegible. His fingers hurt, so he finds it difficult and painful to write, yet he was signing the book for other people.

Below (reduced in size), six courageous men who were awarded the Victoria Cross, the top British award for bravery, in this case in World War 1.

Norman. D. Holbrook.
Lieut: Comdr: R.N.

Gordon Campbell
Captain. R-L.

FRobert Lee Captain
Royal Fusiliers

EB. PF Towse.
Capt. the G or Cor. Highlders.

RECruickshank
Private — London Scottish

A. Martin Leake.
Lieut: Colonel. R.A.M.C

Compare these signatures of classical performers with those of the pop musicians and singers on pages 76-77.

1. Henry Wood
Co-founder of the famous Promenade Concerts in London.

2. Sir Malcolm Sargent
Conductor of the Hallé, Liverpool and BBC Symphony Orchestras.

3. Benjamin Britten
Baron Britten of Aldeburgh, composer, pianist, conductor.

5. Benno Moiseiwitsch,
Russian born pianist who took British nationality.

6. Sir Charles Groves
Conductor.

7. Sir Michael Tippett,
Composer.

8. Colin Davis,
Conductor.

9. Sir Simon Rattle,
Conductor.

10. Vladimir Ashkenazy

11. James Galway,
Flautist

12. Dame Janet Baker,
Mezzo-soprano.

13. Sir Adrian Boult,
Conductor, BBC Symphony Orchestra.

14. Sir John Barbirolli,
Conductor, cellist

15. Sir Thomas Beecham,
Conductor, London Philharmonic Orchestra, artistic director, Covent Garden.

16. Dame Kiri Te Kanawa,
New Zealand born soprano.

1. Sir Cliff Richard
When he was with The Shadows.

2. Garry Glitter

3. Elton John

4. Peter Andre

5. Keith Duffy, Boyzone

6. Lee Brennan, 911

7. The Spice Girls

8. Nigel Kennedy

The brilliant classical violinist. His signature seems more pop than classical.
Compare all these signatures with those on pages 74-75.

1. **Kingsley Amis**

2. **Bridgid Brophy**

3. **Harold Pinter**

4. **Tom Stoppard**
An original signature, it looks a bit like a boot!

5. **Jilly Cooper**
The 'Jilly's is strong, but 'Cooper' fades away.

6. **Roald Dahl**

7. **Melvyn Bragg**
Not legible.

8. **Jeffrey Archer**
Lord Archer's large signature. Could he be archer?

9. **Doris Lessing**

10. **Enid Blyton**
(1897-1968). Prolific chidren's author.

11. John Fowles

12. Malcolm Bradbury

13. G.K. Chesterton
(1874-1936). He studied art at the
Slade. A stylised signature.

14. C.S Forester
(1899-1966).

15. John Buchan
(1875-1940)

16. Thomas Hardy
(1840-1928).

17. Rudyard Kipling
(1865-1936).

18. Sir James Barrie
(1860-1937).

20. G.A. Henty
(1832-1902).

21. George Bernard Shaw
(1856-1950). The Anglo-Irish dramatist was quite keen on striking out verbally.

Ƹ. Pasteur

1. Louis Pasteur
(1822-1895), French bacteriologist.

Joseph Lister

2. Joseph Lister
(1827-1912), Professor of Surgery, pioneer of antiseptics.

Rx ad ʒ viii

Sig The. Gargle

To be used 3 times a day.

Arthur Conan Doyle
M D

3. Sir Arthur Conan Doyle
(1859-1930), creator of Sherlock Holmes. What wonderful writing.

am unable to look after you any longer.

Yours Sincerely

Dr. Ian Farmer

4.
Signature of a modern G.P. who was unable to continue treating a patient because she was a heavy smoker.

Ff Nov . 1953.   *C. G. Jung .*

5. Carl Gustav Jung

(1875-1961), Swiss psychiatrist, founder of analytical psychology.

Yours sincerely truly

6. Alfred Adler

Adler .

(1870-1937), psychologist who inscribed importance to the will to dominate and the inferiority complex. He has a small signature.

Yours sincerely,

7. Prison psychiatrist.

A very wound up,frustrated 'Public Image'.

DR. GEORGE BACH, Psychologist,
Author of "Creative Aggression"

8. Illegible signature.

Sigmund Freud

9.. Sigmund Freud

(1856-1939), founder of psychoanalysis. Large L/Z down into the instinctive unconscious.

1. Sir Peter Scott

British ornithologist and artist. His signature flies upwards.

2. Ian Prestt

Former Director General of the Royal Society for the Protection of Birds. Another upward flight.

3. Eric Hoskins

Wildlife photographer. He was attacked by an owl he was photographing and lost an eye. If you look at the 'E' leftwards, it looks like an art deco face!

4. Jonathan Porritt

Environmental journalist.

5. Thor Heyerdahl

Norwegian anthropologist and explorer, famed for his journey of the raft Kon Tiki.

6. Gerald Durrell

Writer and wildlife enthusiast, his writing helped finance his zoo in Jersey.

7. John Aspinall

An original signature, clever but illegible. A self-confessed gambler, he finances his zoos in the South of England, Howletts and Port Lympne, from the profits of his casinos. He breeds endangered species to return to the wild, as did Gerald Durrell.

8. Sir Francis Chichester

British adventurer who sailed single–handed round the world; great momentum and follow–through.

9. Robin Knox Johnston

Also a lone sailor, he seems more motivated by a high U/Z; he has high aspirations, is on more of a crusade.

10. Julian Pettifer

Active wildlife journalist, he travels at great speed.

11. David Bellamy

British TV star, wildlife and conservation enthusiast, he enjoys publicity. His signature has become inflated, but has a small M/Z.

12. Sir Charles Darwin

(1809–1882), famous for his theory of natural selection and book *The Origin of the Species*.

Note the uncanny similarity of the Chairman's signature and the Company Logo.

 **G.R.A. Property Trust Limited**

WHITE CITY STADIUM, WOOD LANE,
LONDON W12 7RU TELEPHONE: (01) 743 0152

Yours sincerely

1. **Greyhound Racing Association Property Trust Limited.**

Yours sincerely,

2. **Pilgrim Air Limited.**

Yours Sincerely

3.
The signature of a pilot who was involved in a crash. it seems to have made an impact on his 'Public Image'.

4.
A pilot, aptly named. The paraph
under his signature is a perfect outline of a jet.

5.
The fascinating signature of a helicopter pilot.

6. Neil A Armstrong,
Astronaut.

7. Wilbur Wright
and his brother Orville were American pioneers of flying and made the first
powered flight.

Are these signatures examples of how a name, which can give rise to teasing, can influence the writer unconsciously?

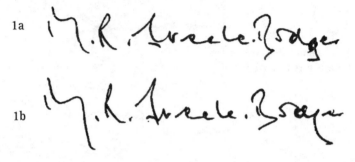

1a & b. The two signatures above were written at different times, but the 'bodge' appears in the same word each time, it is not in the structure, but superimposed on it.

Yours sincerely,

C.P. Hook

2.

The second down stroke on the 'H' has a small hook, the diagonal crossing stroke has a hook and the 'k' is well-hooked. Probably this is all unconscious.

Yours sincerely,

Fr.Alan Fudge.

3.

It could be said that the 'F' is fudged. A dictionary definition of 'to fudge' is to make or adjust in a clumsy way. However, this writer is a holy man. Could it be said that he has superimposed the sign of the cross?

4. Simon Tidy

His signature does not live up to his name.

Yours sincerely

Simon Tidy

5. Percy Thrower

A countryman, perhaps he is casting a fishing line.

6. Sir Randolph Quirk

Could one describe the movement in the capital 'R' as a quirk? A quirk is an unexpected twist or turn; one also talks of a quirk of fate. The former is applicable.

President, The British Academy

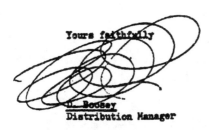

7.

The distribution manager of the International Exhibition Co-operative Wine Society Ltd has surely heard all the jokes about his name dozens of times. I wonder if the jokers have seen his signature, surely written in self-defence?*

*This item first appeared in the 'Peterborough' column of the London *Daily Telegraph*.

1. Anatole France

(1844–1924), French writer. His philosophy was tolerant: 'a person is born a believer or not as he is born blond or brunette; beliefs are only personal opinions'. He reaches up with his 't' cross and curves in three directions, which often indicates humour. At th end of the last 'e' he goes down into the depths, perhaps to trawl up ideas for his books. He won the Nobel Prize for literature in 1921.

2. Robespierre

(1758–1794), French leader at the time of the Revolution. Orphaned at seven, he and his brother were brought up by a maiden aunt.

3. John Drinkwater

(1882–1937), English dramatist and poet: beautiful downwards, swinging curves.

6. Irene Handl

Actress, reaching out.

4. Johann Wolfgang von Goethe

(1749–1832), German poet and dramatist, interested in mysticism and the supernatural.

5. Leo Delibes

(1847–1914), French composer of light opera and ballet.

1. Fred Perry
British, Wimbledon Champion for three years running.

2. Martina Navratilova
Czech/American tennis player, wonderful athlete, Wimbledon Champion a record number of times.

3. Virginia Wade
British, Wimbledon Champion, one of the very few.

4. Mark Cox
British Davis Cup player.

5. Bjorn Borg
Swedish Champion and winner of Wimbledon. His very individualistic style of play, top spinning the ball, is mirrored in his signature.

Plenty of symbolism in these signautres, goal posts and balls etc., but only the writers can throw light on the significance by observing when their signatures start to develop these movements.

Here are two pages of world-class golfers, so there are plenty of good swings! Golf is not a team game but a game for individuals. It requires great determination, the desire to win, physical fitness, self-reliance, self-discipline , self-confidence , great precision and concentration. We know these players have these qualities, but here we are looking at their 'Public Images'.

1. Nick Faldo
Legible, good sense of identity, but a large inflated loop (a sex symbol, or a money bag?) dominates his signature.

2. Ray Floyd
Legible, small; he does not seek publicity.

3. Fred Couples
Very similar.

4. Chip Beck
This is the smallest signature. He dislikes publicity.

5. Tom Kite
Again relatively small. The bottom of the 'T' seems to be developing into a loop.

6. Paul Azinger
Legible, has a huge inflated loop in the U/Z. It looks like a club head.

7. Colin Montgomerie
Very individualistic, angular, large M/Z. He is on a different wavelength to the other players. His golf seems like a crusade.

8. Ian Woosnam

Fairly legible, and then a huge, inflated scoop.

9. Seve Ballesteros

'Seve' is swallowed up by a large loop or sex symbol, but Ballesteros is unaffected.

10. Jose–Maria Olazabal

This appears full of angst; and triangles usually mean frustration.

11. Sam Torrance

Legible, the end stroke of the last 'e' swings round to form a lovely old–fashioned 'wood' or driver.

13. Mark James

An enigma; we don't know who he is.

12. Payne Stewart

The most elegantly coutured golfer. Legible, a sex symbol, he enjoys the limelight.

14. Bernhard Langer

Illegible, lovely rounded writing, no 'hardness'.

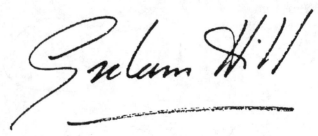

1. Graham Hill
Well known British racing driver, father of Damon Hill.

2. Jackie Stewart
Also a well known British racing driver, now with his own Formula One team.

3. Kenny Roberts
motor bike speed-way champion. This signature rises up almost vertically, 'Kenny' has nice curves but 'Roberts' seems driven by a kind of frenetic antagonism.

4. Henry Cotton
British golf champion, he became famous before the era of TV. No inflated loops.

5. Tony Jacklin
British golfer, 1983.

6.
Tony Jacklin at the height of his career.

7.
Tony Jacklin in 1993. Jackie Stewart crosses through the 'Stewart' with his "t" cross, and underlines the base as if he were trying to keep his 'Public Image' within the road. Tony Jacklin makes a similar stroke over and underlines; perhaps he is trying to stay within the limits of the 'Course'.

8. Arnold Palmer,
American golfer, became more famous because of TV; some inflated loops.

9. Jack Nicklaus
American golfer, most charismatic golfer of all time.

10. Gary Player
South African golfer, who always wore black, a straight forward no nonsense signature, relatively unaffected by publicity.

1. George Best

Very talented but ill-fated footballer. In spite of only two L/Z strokes (in the 'G's of George), he produces four. Two goals equals four posts. They are all crossed through by the line emphasising his name. The story of his life?

2. Paul Gascoigne

Another brilliantly talented player. Here there are only two prescribed strokes, one goal crossed through. A similar story?

3. Sir Bobby Charlton

Another of the 'greats'.

4. Kevin Keegan

A clear, legible signature.

5. Bobby Moore

Captained England in the 1966 World Cup victory. A strong signature, inflated and underlined with a 'pride of material achievement' stroke.

6. Jack Dempsey

A strong signature for a strong boxer.

7. Jimmy Wilde

Was world fly weight boxing champion.

8. Terry Venables
Former England coach. Not an aesthetically attractive signature.

9. Emlyn Hughes
Footballer. Makes an initial flourish, but has small M/Z writing. Does not like publicity.

10. Henry Cooper
Heavy weight boxing champion. A fair-sized, legible signature, Everyone loves our 'Enry.

11. Sir Stanley Matthews
First professional footballer to be knighted. His signature is fluidly versatile, on the ball.

12. Joe Bugner
Was European heavy weight boxing champion. Are they boxing gloves?

1. Dion Dublin

2. Steve Bruce

3. Mark Hughes

8. Paul Parker

4. Andrei Kanchelskis

9. Alex Ferguson

5. Brian Kidd

10. Gary Pallister

6. Kevin Pilkington

7. Colin McKee

11. David May

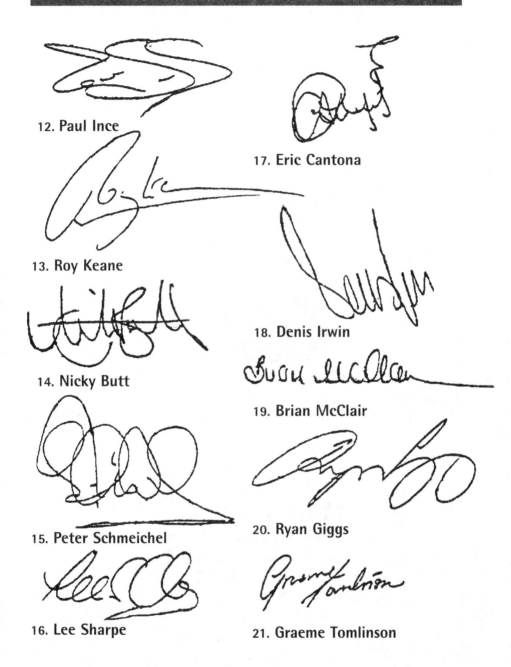

12. Paul Ince

13. Roy Keane

14. Nicky Butt

15. Peter Schmeichel

16. Lee Sharpe

17. Eric Cantona

18. Denis Irwin

19. Brian McClair

20. Ryan Giggs

21. Graeme Tomlinson

9. Is the only signature clearly legible, **19** and **21** are fairly legible, there are eight really large signatures, plenty of dynamic energy. Continually on the move round Europe and the World, very highly paid, macho heroes of the moment, certainly dismissive of other people but inside themselves, insecure, with a certain loss of personal and family identity.

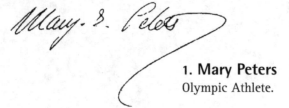

1. Mary Peters
Olympic Athlete.

2. Fatima Whitbread
With her javelin!

3. Pele
Prodigiously gifted footballer helped Brazil to three world cup victories; not surprising to find a ball or two in his signature.

4. Mick Luckhurst
American football star.

5. Mark Spitz
American Olympic swimmer; diving in at speed?

6. Jayne Torville and Christopher Dean

Exceptionally gifted ice dance champions. He includes a skillfully formed skate as a pedestal.

7. Lester Piggott

Champion Jockey; not a publicity seeker.

J. F. Jackman
Secretary

8. J F Jackman,

Crack shot at Bisley.

9. Houdini

Famous escapiologist every letter and 'i' dot is carefully executed, nothing left to chance.

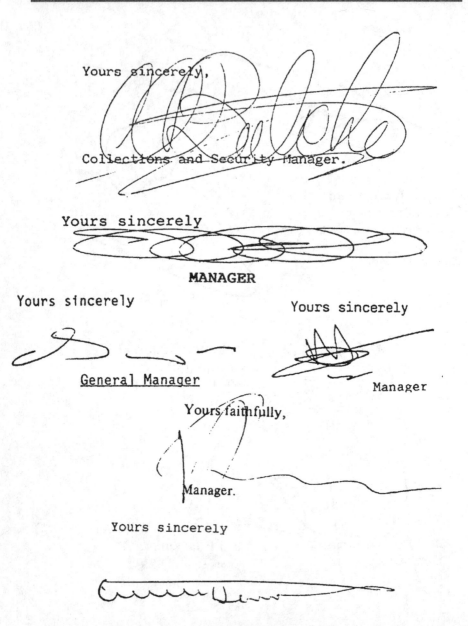

Yours sincerely,

Collections and Security Manager.

Yours sincerely

MANAGER

Yours sincerely

General Manager

Yours sincerely

Manager

Yours faithfully,

Manager.

Yours sincerely

All the illegible signatures on this page are from letters received by clients of the large clearing banks. Are they symptomatic of the loss of public identity suffered by bank employees, perhaps fearful of being responsible, or worried about losing their jobs? In most cases they do not print underneath who they are. This page is worrying. The author wrote to he Chairman of two UK clearing banks: Lloyds and the Midland Bank. The Chairman of Lloyds did not reply, but the Chairman of the Midland (it really is the listening bank) replied with a very legible signature which is reproduced on page 107.

Yours sincerely

MANAGER

Yours sincerely,

Collections and Security Manager.

Yours faithfully,

Manager.

Yours sincerely,

SECURITIES DEPARTMENT   Manager

He said "personally speaking I like to see a legible signature at the bottom of any correspondence addressed to me".

The object of writing this book is to draw attention to the difference between signatures earlier this century and the loss of public identity in today's signatures. There is a real need to inspire people not to be dismissive of themselves and who they are; to inspire them to put some individual pride and design into their 'Public Image', even if it is abbreviated for speed.

Date 28/02/97

AMOUNT OF POUNDS IN WORDS						PENCE AS IN FIGURES	
ZERO	ZERO	ZERO	ZERO	ONE	FOUR	ZERO	£ **140.03**
MILLIONS	HUNDRED THOUSANDS	TEN THOUSANDS	THOUSANDS	HUNDREDS	TENS	UNITS	

This warrant should be presented for payment through a banker within six months or, if not, returned to the Registrar for verification.

The background contains eraser sensitive inks.
U V protected.

A/C PAYEE ONLY

1

1. A dividend cheque sent out by the Unit Trust department of a well-known clearing bank. It has a completely illegible signature, identical to the one received the year before. This is meaningless and only appears as a reassurance to the receiver.

Yours sincerely

HAZEL YOUNG, Manager, Regional Operations

2a

2. The trend appears to be widespread. AA Home Insurance renewal form 1995 2a.(above) has a clear, legible signature. Underneath the manager's name is printed clearly, providing a name to get in touch with. 2b.(below) The signature on the same form in 1997 is illegible. The manager's identity is lost; we have only a computer I.D.

Yours sincerely

For AA Insurance

2b

1. Anita Roddick
Chief Executive, The Body Shop

2. Richard Branson
Virgin Group

3. Christine Hancock
General Secretary, Royal College of Nursing

4. Alan Yentob
Controller, BBC1 Television

5. Harvey Goldsmith
Chief Executive, Allied Entertainments Group

6. Sir Colin Marshall
Chairman, British Airways plc

7. Baroness Chalker of Wallasey

Between them they must have signed thousands of documents and letters, yet their signatures are all legible.

1. Lord Hanson

2. Gregory Hutchings
Chairman, Tomkins.

3. W.H. Smith
Founder of the firm.

4. Joseph Rank

5. Val Duncan

6. Anthony Tennant
Former Chairman of Guinness

7. Alex Bernstein
Former Chairman of Granada

8. Sir William Purves
Former Chairman, Midland Bank

9. Sir Monty Finniston

10. William Mather

11. Anthony Tuke
Former Chairman, Barclays Bank

12. Howard Thomas
Former Chairman, Thames Television

1. Robert Maxwell

2. James Goldsmith

3. Jim Slater

4.
Former Chairman of British Gas; the top 'E' looks like a gas flame

5.
Chairman with an illegible signature, but every letter is represented. It looks like a smoking hand grenade.

6. Ernest Saunders
Former Guinness Chairman. Legible, cultured, capitals high, small M/Z.

7.
Chairman, a powerful, rather complicated 'Public Image'.

8.

Managing Director. 'Tim' is legible, but he is not so keen on his surname: it has turned into a loop.

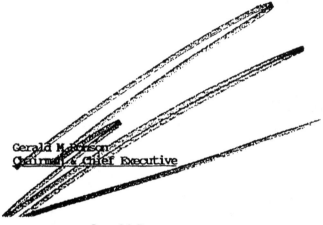

9. Gerald Ronson

10.

Deputy Chief Executive, a 'cultivated' signature, illegible, sophisticated, aesthetic panache.

11.

High Tech Manager with a high tech signature.

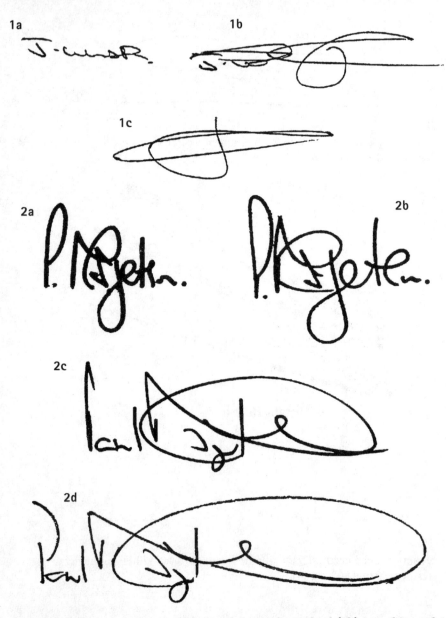

1a. Signature of a receipts clerk. It subsequently evolved (1b) into this; and then (1c) into this. If he has to sign so many receipts, why can he not initial them, or use a stamp which would better represent him and his company? 2a. A fairly legible signature. 2b. the surname has inflated. 2c. A first name has appeared, the surname has inflated, spread, become illegible. Inflation can occur from pride emanating from success, or when people over–compensate to redeem what they see as a personal disadvantage. 2d. The surname has become more inflated.

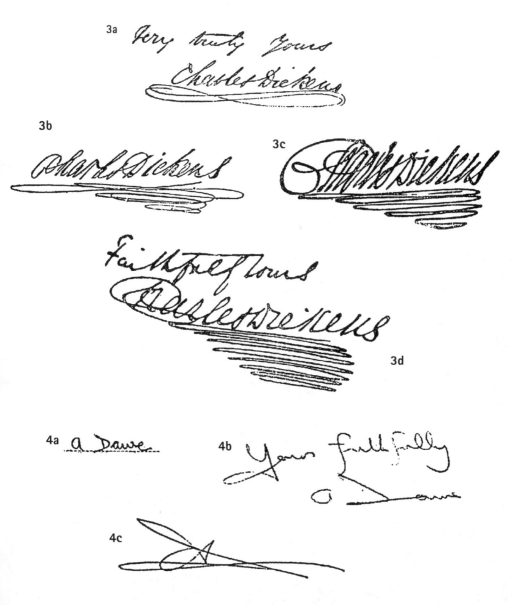

3. Charles Dickens (1812–1870), English novelist, a best seller for over 100 years. **3a.** He underlines his signature with two loops in 1831. **3b.** It is underlined with four loops in 1832. **3c.** It is underlined with five loops in 1838, becoming a pedestal to reinforce his importance. **3d.** It has got seven loops in 1859. Most of his novels had been written by then. He was editor of All the Year Round. His signature is beginning to lean downwards. His father was imprisoned for debt in 1824 and Dickens had to work in a blacking factory. Perhaps this bitter experience in his youth made him reinforce his own "Public Standing". **4a.** A nice clear signature. **4b.** Still legible. **4c.** Illegible, following the modern trend.

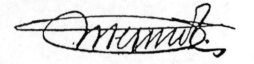

1. Jean Mermoz
French air ace of World War 1. His name is protected by the outline of a plane.

2. Company Chairman
Illegible. This person needs all-round overhead cover

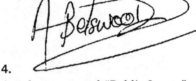

3.
Completely enveloped, like a magic circle.

4.
Another protected "Public Image".

5. "Appointed Bees Officer"
He needs complete protection from the bees and their owners.
His visits are not always welcome.

6. Joseph N. Niepce
1765-1833. Physicist.

7.
Electronics publisher
Puts a circuit round himself.

8. Walpole

Nominally first Prime Minister of Britain, he had to withstand opposition from MPs.

9. Count Zeppelin

He brings the end stroke back, making his signature rather like the airship he designed

10.

Thoroughly encircled and re-encircled.

11. Victoria de los Angeles

The beautiful singer wraps herself up in a treble clef.

12.

Here the stroke, swinging leftwards, crosses through the signature.

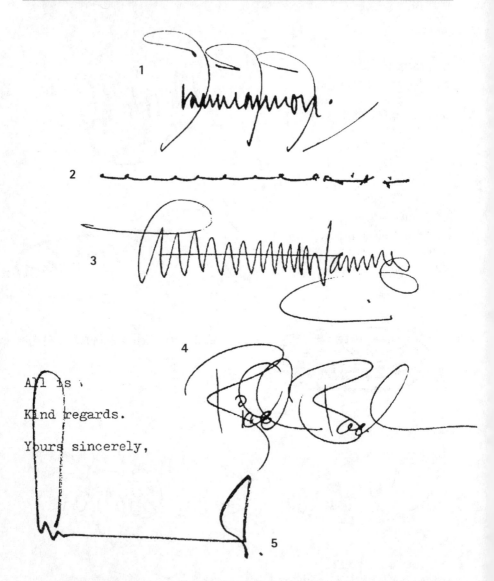

1. The only person who can shed any light on why a signature developed like this is the writer himself. We can only guess that his "Public Image" is dominated by something which involves the number three. Could it be golf or fishing three times a week? Or is he involved with some sort of engineering machinery? 2. The signature of a former secretary of the Henley Regatta. If you look at the signature from left to right, there is one stroke for the end of the boat, then eight oars, all rowing. After this there are a few confused dots and dashes – staccato instructions coming from the cox to his crew. Finally, there is the cox at the right with his controls. 3. An army officer's signature. 4. Richard Bach, author of *Jonathan Livingston Seagull*: up in the clouds. 5. A solicitor: looks like an empty bed.

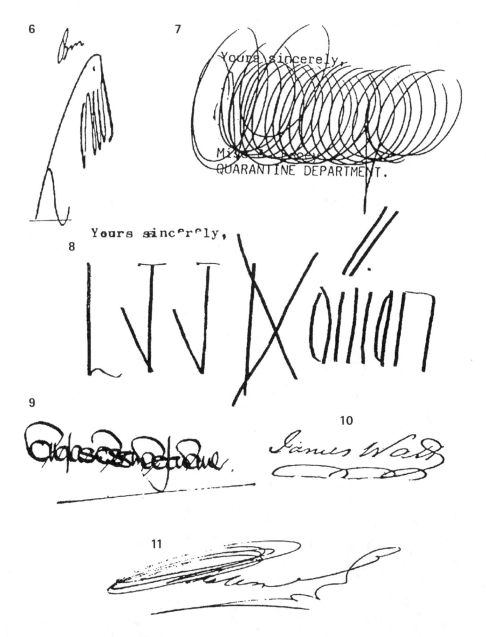

6. Louis XVI, King of France. A sad and very unusual signature, which looks like a praying mantis. 7. A signature from a cat's boarding establishment, reinforced with rolls of wire. 8. An applicant for a job in computers. 9. This one must take a very long time to complete. 10. James Watt, Scottish engineer completed the engine he designed in 1775. It looks as if he is steaming along, leaving a trail of smoke. 11. The signature of the director of a tobacco company. He appears to be smoking away.

1. **Alexandre Dumas**

(1824-1895) French playwright,
known as Dumas fils.
Beautiful, artistic curves.

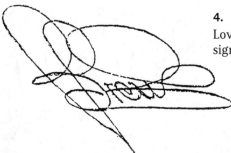

2.
Illegible, slightly crossed-through.

3.
Very flattened M/Z and angles

4.
Lovely curves, but he does cross his
signature right through

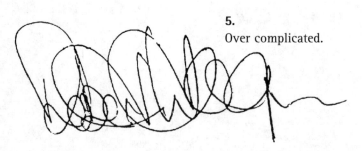

5.
Over complicated.

6.
Very curvaceous, but it looks like someone
riding a bicycle.

7. Joachim Murat
(1767-1815) French Marshall.
He is protecting his back.

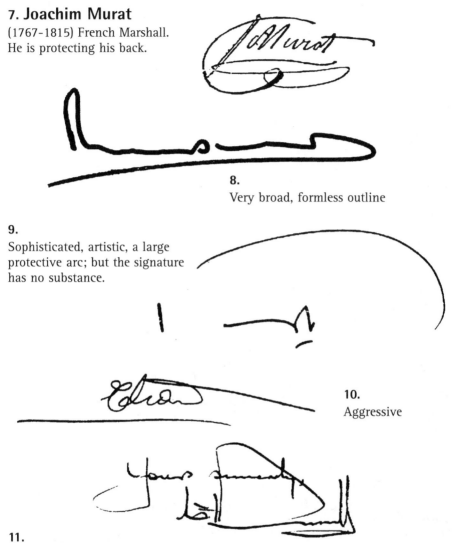

8.
Very broad, formless outline

9.
Sophisticated, artistic, a large
protective arc; but the signature
has no substance.

10.
Aggressive

11.
It looks as if this writer's overriding interest is sailing; even the rudder is there.

12.
This writer worked at one time with illuminated manuscripts. Enthralled by
their beauty, she has incorporated some of their scrolls and embellishments
in her signature.

Another two pages of unusual signatures. It is important to say yet again that only the writers themselves can have insight into how and why they developed in this way.Through this insight they could find their way back to who they really are. 8 and 14 are protecting their 'Public Image'. 6 and 12 are just too large. they have forgotten that 'blessed are the meek, for they shall inherit the earth'. 2 and 13 are crossing themselves out. If only they could underline their signatures instead, they would respect their Public Image, and in so doing give more respect to themselves.

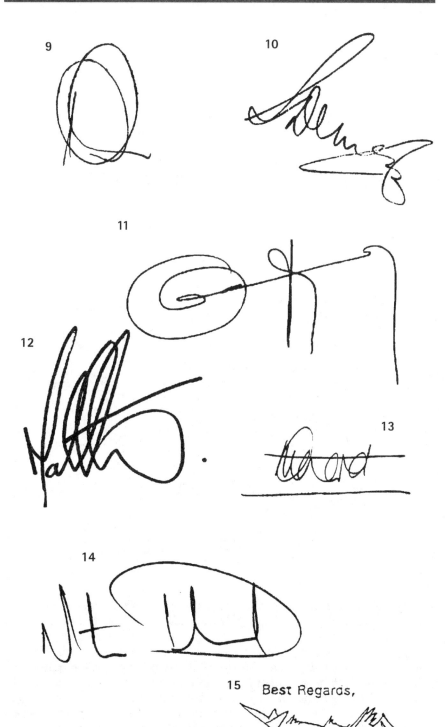

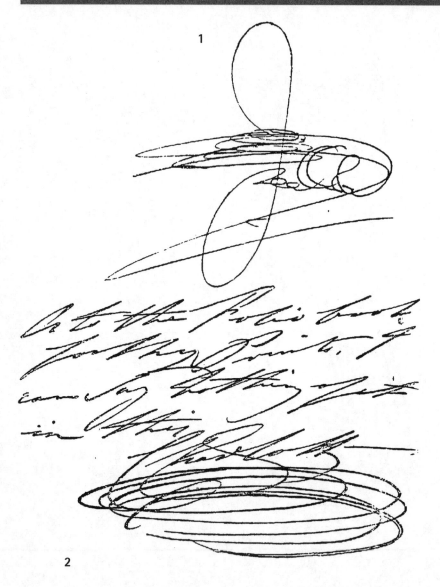

These signatures emanate from discomfort and frustration. Perhaps writers who gradually adopt this style of signature can think back to how it started and try to unravel.

2. is the signature of Princess Charlotte (1796–1817), the luckless only child of George IV and Princess Caroline of Brunswick. George, formerly Prince Regent, married Princess Caroline when offered some financial inducement to settle his debts. The marriage, as expected, was a disaster. The King even refused to let his wife attend his coronation. It is not surprising that Princess Charlotte felt everything was against her. She married King Leopold of Belgium, but died the next year having their first child.

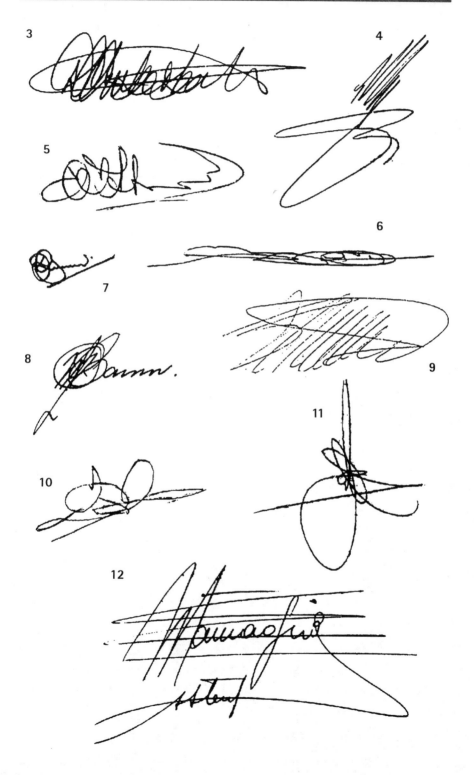

THE SIGNATURES OF DAVID CORNWELL/JOHN LE CARRÉ

Permutations on the signature of David Cornwell, who is a well-known author under the name John Le Carré. The question is 'Does he feel more at home as John Le Carré or David Cornwell'? These are all free, legible signatures. David flows, but Cornwell has lost some of its fluency. It seems that the dangerous, secret world of John Le Carré has taken him over!

CHANGING SIGNATURES OVER THE YEARS

1. Rudolf Nureyev

The former leading dancer of the Kirov Ballet. His signature soon after he defected to the West in1961. A bouquet of ballet shoes?

2.

Nureyev's signature many years later, greatly changed by his high profile social status in the West.

3. Peter Gabriel

Musician, singer, pop star, entrepreneur, initiator of 'Womad'. This is his signature in 1961.

4.

Peter Gabriel's signature in 1963, rising up optimistically.

5.

Peter Gabriel's signature in 1993: fairly small, legible, very simplified, sophisticated, not that of a publicity seeker.

CHANGING SIGNATURES ON DIFFERENT OCCASIONS

[handwritten signature] : reserved for boring things like prescriptions, cheques, etc.

[handwritten signature: Jonathan Brooklin] : a personal letter using my christian name – or rather the name by which I am known.

[handwritten signature: Alistair George Johnston] : for pompous documents that are going to end up in some vault or other.

[handwritten initials] : A.J.J. my initials!

6.

A doctor in general practice, who has been High Sheriff of the County, explains the four different versions of his 'Public Image' and their suitability for his different roles.

1a. Laurence Olivier

Early in his career.

1b. Sir Laurence Olivier

At the height of his talent.

1c. Lord Olivier

In his later years.

2a. Desmond Morris

In 1971.

2b.

His signature in 1976. He became well-known after the publication of *The Naked Ape* and *The Human Zoo*. Is this the effect of publicity on his 'Public Image'?

2c

In 1994 he has reverted to his former signature, though it has become larger and more pronounced.

3a.

Sir Jeffrey M. Sterling

The Chairman of P & O's signature in 1987.

3b.

His signature in 1988, the year the cross channel ferry Herald of Free Enterprise went down. Is it just a coincidence that his signature swings over to the left?

3c.

His signature in 1989, back on course.

4a.

Katherine Whitehorn

The well known journalist in 1971.

4b.

Her signature in 1976.

126

1a. Napoleon Buonaparte
When he was a Captain in the army.

1b.
Later, as Emperor, he signed Napoleon.

2a. Adolf Hitler
His signature in 1933, before he became Chancellor of Germany.
There is a downward stroke crossing the 'f' of Adolf.

2b.
By 1938, Adolf has become an outline, with the same downward stroke on the 'f'; but now another cross stroke appears on the 'H' of Hitler, and the whole word fall down more steeply.

3a. Benito Mussolini
Before he became dictator of Italy.

3b.
When in power, his signature became just Mussolini. It is getting larger as he becomes more powerful.

127

4a. Richard Nixon

In 1959 his signature has plenty of vigour and drive. But notice the stroke of the X is used to cross the name through.

4b.

n 1969 President Nixon's signature shows severe shrinkage in the M/Z letters.

4c.

A third signature: further M/Z shrinkage.

4d.

In the fourth signature the M/Z has disappeared all together and the crossing through is more marked. This is Watergate.

Above are the signatures of four generations of the Churchill family: Lord Randolph Churchill, Sir Winston Churchill, his son Randolph Churchill and grandson Winston Churchill. Notice how all four end with a simplified form of the letter 'l' and how the second 'l' is shorter than the first. They all feel the need for some reinforcement under the end of the signature. Lord Randolph, Sir Winston's father, even adds the date.

2a. Sir David Attenborough
World-famous naturalist and broadcaster.

2b. Lord Attenborough
Richard, David's equally talented and successful brother; film actor, director and politician. He has a similar width and writing style, but more complex L/Z loops.

[signature: J. Chamberlain]

2a. Joseph Chamberlain
British politician.

[signature: Neville Chamberlain]

2b. Neville Chamberlain
His son, who succeeded Stanley Baldwin as Prime Minister.

[signature: Austen Chamberlain]

2c. Sir J Austen Chamberlain
Half-brother of the above.

[signature: Osbert Sitwell]

[dated: Oct. 1927]

[signature: Edith Sitwell]

3a & b. Osbert Sitwell and Edith Sitwell
Brother and sister, both were highly individual poets and writers. The family formed a closely-knit clan.

4a. Sir Malcolm Campbell

Reached 301mph in his famous car Bluebird in Utah. In 1939 he broke the then world water speed record at 141.7mph.

4b. Donald Campbell

Son of the above. He, too, broke the world water speed record, reaching 202mph. Whilst attempting to reach 300mph his boat disintegrated and he was killed.

5a. Lord Forte

Founder of the Forte hotel chain.

5b. Rocco Forte

Son of the above, he fought unsuccessfully to avoid the company being taken over by Granada.

1. Jonathan Dimbleby

Enigmatic, versatile, interesting. He uses the same unusual structure to the Capital 'D' as his brother.

2. David Dimbleby

A stylised signature, large, legible, angular, upright; reserved, solid, unshakeable; huge sweep leftwards in the L/Z.

3. Jacqueline Kennedy

Her writing slopes slightly to the left, has a sophisticated style; cold, reserved, interested in history and the past.

4. John F Kennedy

Strong right slant writing, more active, outgoing, warm, large L/Z, earthy.

Douglas M. Hogg

5. The Rt Hon Sir Douglas M. Hogg KC
MP 1872-1950, a really lovely signature.

Yours sincerely :

6. The Rt Hon Quintin M. Hogg
Son of the above, MP, Attorney General, Lord Chancellor, Viscount Hailsham: a stylised, very legible signature.

Hailsham

Douglas Hogg

7. Rt Hon Douglas Hogg
Son of Viscount Hailsham, MP, Minister of Agriculture. His signature is large, right slant, angular, illegible, following the modern trend.

Two signatures from Klara Roman's Book and one from a book by John Symonds

1. This comes from Klara Roman's book *Handwriting, a Key to personality.* It is the Initial letter of the signature of a police officer who, in a sudden rage, killed his wife because, as he explained, she took too much of the quilt for herself.

2. This signature, from Klara Roman's book, is that of an American Justice of the Peace. One of his jobs was to perform wedding services. He was unmarried himself and lived alone. His first initial was 'J'. Notice how the very symbolic U/Z floats away, cut off, disassociated from the extremely flattened M/Z. Then there is an enormously inflated L/Z loop to the 'J', showing excessive imagination invested in unconscious instincts and fantasy, which is incompatible with the crushed M/Z. When this celibate, respected, civil servant died, officials were dumbfounded to be confronted with a vast collection of obscene pin-ups pervading and spreading over the walls of his bedroom.

3. This signature comes from the book *The Great Beast* by John Symonds. It is Aleister Crowley

1. Overpowering German signature from the early 20th century. Very angular, with U/Z emphasis and pointed loops and scrolls. 2. Similar date, again German, the L/Z is emphasised with seven triangles. 3. Algernon Charles Swinburne (1837–1909). This English poet is unsurpassed for the sensual verbal music in his verse. It is said that 'his poems can still disturb, but no longer shock'. This signature has a smeary, murky, unwholesome atmosphere; the thick stroke is loaded with sensuality. 4. Thomas Cochran. His signature has the same muddy, unwholesome ambience, but it slopes to the left, so he is influenced by the past and what has gone before. He was found guilty of a singularly unpleasant sex murder.

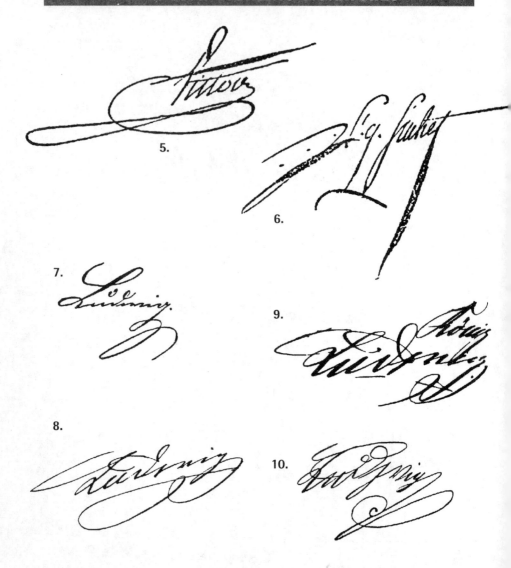

5. & 6. Two Marshalls created by Napoleon. 5 seems well armed and protected. 6 has a fearsome aspect to it, striking out and down. 7,8,9 & 10. These are all signatures of Ludwig II of Bavaria (1845–1886), patron of Wagner. He inherited a taste for artistic extravagance and built a number of fairy tale castles . One, the Linde Hof, is encrusted with ornamentation inside, for example elaborate mirrors and chandeliers, with insufficient space to dilute their impact. He had a garden house with a 'Peacock Throne' where he presided over an imaginary kingdom. Sadly, these signatures show a progressive descent into confusion and madness. He was ultimately found drowned in Lake Strainberg. However, his castles have become great tourist attractions, so he has left his country a legacy for all time.

The signatures on this and the next page produce a sense of well-being.

Flora Robson

1796.

G. Washington

Aug 1922.

Thomas Hardy.

Arthur Conan Doyle
M.D.

Humphrey Lyttelton

Antony Hopkins*

Kenneth Kendall

*The composer and pianist, not the actor.
The actor's signature is on page 58.

Conclusion

Mary E Jeans, aged 100

The legible signature of Mary E Jeans, aged 100, is the final illustration. So now what are we to make of all this? The reason for writing this book was to throw some light on the drastic deterioration of signatures in the last quarter of the 20th Century. Perhaps we should go back in history and see what drives humankind. Clever, inquisitive, an inveterate explorer, with an inbuilt urge to go further, find out more, never satisfied with what he has achieved.

One of early man's first remarkable discoveries was the ability to 'make fire', to keep his extended family group warm. It also gave him light, enabled him to cook food and acted as a deterrent to potential predators.

Another major development was the construction of the wheel. This extended the use of his legs for covering distances and the 'water wheel' extended the use of his arms for lifting water.

His ability to communicate within his family group with various sounds and gestures, gradually over the millenia, developed into written signs and pictures, (see page 2 and 3). This then developed into language and a phonetic alphabet which could be written down, then printed. Through the printed word his thoughts could be conveyed across distances, extending his influence to other destinations. Mankind developed this ability independently in different parts of the world where there was no communication. Hundreds and hundreds of different languages developed of their own volution.

He extended his hearing and his ability to communicate, first with telephones and then radio, world wide. He also extended his sight with binoculars, telescopes and now television. It is as if this extension of his limbs and senses was a gradual 'built in ' programme of enhancing his abilities and globalising his achievements.

History tells us of the major upheavals to society caused by the industrial revolution. Machinery extended the manufacture of previously hand-crafted items, carriages were superseded by cars, buses, trains, which increased countrywide mobility and then air travel increased mobility world wide.

Now we are all, internationally caught up in the major upheaval of the electronic revolution. Mankind has discovered a way of electronically enhancing and extending the brain. Information can be universal and world wide, crossing barriers. We have all become citizens of the world.

You may now ask, what on earth has this to do with signatures? So we must get back to handwriting. Your writing and your signature can change remarkably throughout your life, mirroring maturity, progress, health, ups and downs and major events. Pages 123 to 126 illustrate changes in signatures.

Reginald Piggott, in his book, *Handwriting, a National Survey,* based on 25,000 examples of handwriting, divides the writings into professional groups. He then produces tables on various aspects of handwriting. One table is on 'Legibility'. This is divided into four groups, which range from (a), almost illegible, very difficult to read, to (d), completely legible.

In Group (a) Piggott finds that his Professional Group 'Scientists and Research Workers', contains the most illegible writings. (Doctors were in another group) Whereas in Group (d) the most legible writings were found in the Professional Group 'H.M. Services, all ranks, men and women', Closely followed by the group headed 'Manual Workers'.

Earlier in this book, two main reasons were put forward as to why people take the trouble to write and yet write completely illegibly. One was that the writers did not care if the recipient could read the written message or not. This is a complete lack of thought or respect for the receiver. However, it could apply to academic research scientists, who may work in a very select field, becoming rarefied in the mystique of their speciality, only communicating with people in the same orbit. They can have some disdain or lack of touch with ordinary people. There is some intellectual superiority in being incomprehensible. It could also apply to people who are so self-centred and puffed up with their own importance that they have very little regard at all for others. These could be in any professional group.

In Piggott's survey, the most legible writing was found in Professional groups where there was discipline, a strong social framework, and a sense of belonging to a group.

The armed forces are a tight knit community. Their success is based on fitness, discipline, team work, being expert at their particular skills and knowing their place in the hierachy. On active service they are dependent, for their lives, on each other and build up a sense of comradeship, singing as they march along, each individual becomes an essential part of the whole. Except on active service, they have a sense of security, they have no major personal worries about housing, food, clothing, this is all provided. They are motivated to have respect for their officers and respect for themselves, in their efficiency and appearance.

The second group of legible writers were 'Manual Workers'. When Piggott undertook his Survey in 1954, factory workers, miners and others, had comradeship on the job, and where they lived, close by, were tight knit communities.

The second reason for illegibility was that the writers did not want the recipient to be able to read the message. In a small way this can be illustrated by a writer. He comes to a word and is unsure of the spelling, so he decides to blur the letters and make the word illegible as a 'cover up '. With a signature this can occur when the writer does not want to divulge his actual name. It can also occur when someone does not want to be ultimately responsible for the letter he has to write, so he makes himself anonymous.

With the increasing 'fast food', 'fast money', fast turnover of news and technology, the environment of ordinary people has become increasingly insecure, uncertain and rootless. It is not surprising that their 'Public Images' have been undermined.

The pervading problem in society today seems the break up of the extended family group and the tight knit communities. People move with jobs. There is a lack of self-discipline, and a general lack of respect for parents, politicians, bosses, the church. Who is there to look up to? Lack of respect for others can be lack of respect for yourself. In the writing of signatures, we have a visual record of what is happening. Things have to start at the bottom line, and we all depend on each other, we are all in this together. We are all of the world and belong to the world. So if you are one of the myriads of people who make illegible signatures like these:-

Why not make a start to realise who you are and what you stand for, redesign your signature, make it legible and underline it, have some respect for yourself. This will generate an internal 'feel good' factor. If you think positively, it attracts positive events. Perhaps you can influence your friends as well, the future depends on us all.

Jane Paterson

BIBLIOGRAPHY

The Philosophy of Handwriting, Don Felix de Salamanca Chatto & Windus, 1879
The Handwriting of the Kings and Queens of England, W.J. Hardy,
   The Religious   Society, 1893
Autograph Collecting, Henry T. Scott, L. Upcott Gill, London, 1894
The Story of the Alphabet, Edward Clodd, George Newnes Ltd, London, 1900
The Language of Handwriting, Richard Dimsdale Stocker, Routledge, 1904
Character Indicated by Handwriting, Rosa Baughan, Rider, London, 1905
Analysis of Handwriting, Hans,.J. Jacoby, Allen & Unwin, London, 1939
What Your Handwriting Shows, Robert Saudek, J. Werner Laurie, London, 1939
Self-Knowledge Through Handwriting, Hans J. Jacoby, Dent, London, 1941
Handwriting, the Key to Successful Living, Herry O. Teltscher, Putnam,
   New York, 1942
Handwriting and Marriage, Dr Eric Singer, Rider, London , 1953
Handwriting, a Key to Personality, Klara G. Roman, Routledge, 1954
Handwriting, A National Survey, Reginald Piggott, Allen & Unwin, 1958
Pens and Personalities, Josef Ranald, Vision, 1959
Handwriting, an Analysis through its Symbolism, Rudolph S. Hearns, Vantage,
   New York, 1966
Handwriting Tells, Nadya Olyanova, Peter Owen, London 1969
Four Hundred Years of British Autographs, Ray Rawlins, Dent, London, 1970
Handwriting, Revelation of Self, Dr Herry O. Teltscher, Hawthorn,
   New York, 1971
Grapho-Therapeutics, Paul de Sainte Colombe, Laurida Books, California, 1971
English Royal Signatures, Public Record Office, London, 1973
You and Your Handwriting, Jeanne Heal, Pelham, London, 1973
You are what you write, Huntington Hartford, Macmillan, New York, 1973
Le Guide Marabout de la Graphologie, Anne-Marie Cobbaert,
   Marabout, Verviers 975
Graphology, Monique le Guen, Ariane, 1976
Interpreting Handwriting, Jane Paterson, Macmillan, London, 1976
The Guinness Book of World Autographs, Ray Rawlins, 1977
Know Yourself through your Handwriting, Jane Paterson, Readers Digest,
   London 1978
Naming Names, Adrian Room, Routledge, 1981
Our Names, Ourselves, Mary Lassiter, Heinemann, London, 1983

INDEX OF SIGNATURES

Index of Signatures

Printed in the United States
70369LV00002B/48